jQuery 2.0 Animation Techniques Beginner's Guide

Bring your websites to life with animations using jQuery

Adam Culpepper

Dan Wellman

BIRMINGHAM - MUMBAI

jQuery 2.0 Animation Techniques Beginner's Guide

First published: December 2013

Production Reference: 1171213

Published by Packt Publishing Ltd.
Livery Place
35 Livery Street
Birmingham B3 2PB, UK.
ISBN 978-1-78216-964-2

www.packtpub.com

Cover Image by Jeremy Segal (info@jsegalphoto.com)

Credits

Authors
  Adam Culpepper

  Dan Wellman

Reviewers
  Jeff Byrnes

  Emil Lerch

  Doug Sparling

Acquisition Editors
  Harsha Bharwani

  Akram Hussain

Lead Technical Editors
  Mayur Hule

  Larissa Pinto

Technical Editors
  Iram Malik

  Menza Mathew

  Rahul U. Nair

  Pratish Soman

Project Coordinator
  Anugya Khurana

Proofreaders
  Lauren Harkins

  Elinor Perry-Smith

Indexer
  Mehreen Deshmukh

Production Coordinator
  Shantanu Zagade

Cover Work
  Shantanu Zagade

About the Authors

Adam Culpepper is a frontend web developer who works for Envoc, a software development firm, located in Baton Rouge, Louisiana. He is very active in his community; organizing, founding, and sitting on the board of many industry-related groups and organizations in his area. When he's not reading, writing, working, organizing, or attending a community event, he's spending time with his great friends and family or his girlfriend Amber, his son Aiden and his cat Emma. Adam can be reached at his website (www. adamculpepper.net) or through Twitter (@adamculpepper).

Dan Wellman is an author and web developer based on the South coast of the UK. By day he works alongside some of the most talented people he has had the pleasure of calling colleagues, for a small, yet accomplished digital agency called Design Haus. By night he writes books and tutorials on a range of frontend topics. He is hopelessly addicted to jQuery. His life is enriched by four wonderful children, a beautiful wife, and a close circle of family and friends. This is his fifth book.

I would like to thank the hugely supportive and patient editorial team at Packt, without whom this book would not exist. I would also like to thank the reviewers, especially Ben Nadel and Cyril Pierron, who put aside their own personal projects and dedicated countless hours to ensuring the book's technical accuracy. I'd also like to say a big Hey! to some of my closest friends, in no particular order; Andrew Herman, Steev Bishop, Aaron Matheson, Eamon O'Donoghue, James Zabiela, Mike Woodford, and John Adams.

About the Reviewers

Jeff Byrnes is a software engineer with over 8 years of experience working in web development and operations. Educated as a musician at Berklee College of Music, self-taught as an engineer, he has experience ranges from frontend to backend and systems. HTML5, CSS3, JS, PHP, Git and version control, Puppet, Chef, Vagrant, Bash, Linux, deployment, automation, and analytics; these are all the technologies and skills with which he is experienced and proficient.

Currently, part of the Operations team at EverTrue, Jeff spends his days supporting the engineering team, providing automation, server monitoring and maintenance, workflow improvements, and deployment solutions, as well as providing help desk support to the company at large.

> I'd like to thank Dale Cruse for connecting me with the opportunity to assist with this book's publication, and my better half Leah for supporting me as I worked on it.

Emil Lerch is a technical architect, leading teams to build web-based systems for enterprises since 1995. He lives in Portland, Oregon with his wife Kelly and children Kathryn and Jack. His blog is `http://emilsblog.lerch.org` and he can be reached on twitter `@elerch`.

> My lovely wife and children for giving me the time to help review the book.

Doug Sparling works as a web and mobile software developer for Andrews McMeel Universal, a publishing and syndication company in Kansas City, MO. As long-time employee of the company, he has built everything from the GoComics Android app to registration, ecommerce systems, web services, and various web sites using Ruby on Rails. He's now busy building another site in Rails and porting a Perl-based e-mail system to Go. Some of the AMU properties include GoComics.com, PuzzleSociety.com, Doonesbury.com, and Dilbert.com.

He is also the directory of technology for the small web development firm called New Age Graphics (newage-graphics.com). After creating a custom CMS using C# and ASP.NET, all work has moved to WordPress since WordPress 3.0 was released, eliminating the need to ever run Windows again.

Doug is the author of a popular jQuery plugin, **jClock**.

Doug is a passionate advocate for WordPress and has written several WordPress plugins, can be found on the WordPress.org forums answering questions (and writing sample code) under the username "scriptrunner", and occasionally plays grammar nerd as a volunteer on the WordPress Codex Documentation team.

Other experience includes PHP, JavaScript, jQuery, Erlang, Python, Magento, and Perl. Doug was also the co-author for a Perl book (Instant Perl modules) and is a reviewer for other Packt books, including Mastering Android 3D Game Development and WordPress Web Application Development, as well as The Well Ground Rubyist, 2nd Edition and Learn Android in a Month of Lunches for Manning Publications.

In his less than ample spare time, Doug enjoys spending time with his family. Other passions include photography, writing music, hitting drums and cymbals with sticks, playing briscola, meditation, and watching countless reruns of Firefly, Buffy the Vampire Slayer, and Doctor Who.

Many thanks to Packt for giving me the opportunity to review a book on jQuery.

---

www.PacktPub.com

Support files, eBooks, discount offers and more

You might want to visit `www.PacktPub.com` for support files and downloads related to your book.

Did you know that Packt offers eBook versions of every book published, with PDF and ePub files available? You can upgrade to the eBook version at `www.PacktPub.com` and as a print book customer, you are entitled to a discount on the eBook copy. Get in touch with us at `service@packtpub.com` for more details.

At `www.PacktPub.com`, you can also read a collection of free technical articles, sign up for a range of free newsletters and receive exclusive discounts and offers on Packt books and eBooks.

`http://PacktLib.PacktPub.com`

Do you need instant solutions to your IT questions? PacktLib is Packt's online digital book library. Here, you can access, read and search across Packt's entire library of books.

Why Subscribe?

- ◆ Fully searchable across every book published by Packt
- ◆ Copy and paste, print and bookmark content
- ◆ On demand and accessible via web browser

Free Access for Packt account holders

If you have an account with Packt at `www.PacktPub.com`, you can use this to access PacktLib today and view nine entirely free books. Simply use your login credentials for immediate access.

Table of Contents

Preface

jQuery is a cross-browser JavaScript library designed to simplify the client-side scripting of HTML, and is the most popular JavaScript library in use today. Using the features offered by jQuery, developers are able to create dynamic web pages. This book will act as a resource for you to create animation and advanced special effects in your web applications, by following the easy-to-understand steps mentioned in it.

jQuery 2.0 Animation Techniques Beginner's Guide will allow you to master animation in jQuery to produce slick and attractive interfaces that respond to your visitors' interactions. You will learn everything you need to know about creating engaging and effective web page animations using jQuery. The book uses many examples and explains how to create animations using an easy, step-by-step, beginner's guide approach.

This book provides various examples that gradually build up the reader's knowledge and practical experience in using the jQuery API to create stunning animations. The book starts off by explaining how animations make your user interface interactive and attractive. It explains the various methods used to make the element being animated appear or disappear. It provides a set of steps to create simple animations and show fading animations.

You can later learn how to make complex animations by chaining different effects together as well as how to halt a currently running animation. You will find out how to slide your animation elements and learn to create custom animations that can be complex and specialized.

You will learn how to obtain and set up jQuery UI—the official user interface library for jQuery. This book will tell you how to animate a page's background image, and will teach you how to make images scroll in a certain direction and at a certain speed depending on the movement of the mouse pointer.

What this book covers

Chapter 1, Getting Started, covers the basics including downloading jQuery and setting up a development area, a brief history of animation on the Web, when and where not to use animation, how animation can enhance an interface, and the animation methods exposed by jQuery. A basic example of animation is also covered.

Chapter 2, Image Animation, uses a simple approach to creating an image slider. We then build features into the slider and are left with a script worthy of your next development project.

Chapter 3, Background Animation, takes us through the journey of creating animated background images and background color when our user scrolls down our site. This very subtle animation adds a lot of aesthetic appeal to websites.

Chapter 4, Navigation Animation, covers creative ways to add animation to navigation on our websites. We'll be fading the background color of our web page and smooth scrolling to clicked links on the page.

Chapter 5, Form and Input Animation, focuses on animation that is triggered by our user's interaction with the form. We will guide our users through our form using animations for form validation and to give our form a better experience overall.

Chapter 6, Extending Animations with jQuery UI, looks at the additional effects added by jQuery UI, the official UI library built on top of jQuery. We look at each of the 14 effects as well as covering the easing functions built into the library.

Chapter 7, Custom Animation, focuses on the `animate()` method, which jQuery provides for us as a means of creating custom animations not already predefined. This extremely powerful method allows us to animate almost any CSS-style property to easily create complex and attractive animations.

Chapter 8, Other Popular Animations, looks at some common types of animations found on the web including proximity animations triggered by the mouse pointer, animated headers, and a modern-day equivalent to the marquee element.

Chapter 9, CSS3 Animations, covers how we can use CSS3 to create attractive animations driven by the latest CSS transforms and how jQuery can be used to make the process easier.

Chapter 10, Canvas Animations, looks at the HTML5 canvas element and shows how it can be used to create stunning animations without the use of Flash or other proprietary technologies. The book closes with an in-depth example teaching how to create an interactive game using nothing but HTML and JavaScript.

What you need for this book

To get the most out of this book you should have some knowledge of front-end development, preferably including JavaScript. Experience with jQuery is also preferable, but is not essential as all techniques used in the book are discussed in full.

You should have a computer capable of running the latest browsers and preferably an Internet connection. A code editing development software package will be of help, but again is not essential provided you have a text editor of some kind.

Who this book is for

This book is written for web designers and front-end developers who already have good knowledge of HTML and CSS. While not required, some experience with jQuery or JavaScript is helpful. If you want to learn how to animate the user interface of your web applications with jQuery, then this book is for you.

Conventions

In this book, you will find several headings appearing frequently.

To give clear instructions of how to complete a procedure or task, we use:

Time for action – heading

1. Action 1
2. Action 2
3. Action 3

Instructions often need some extra explanation so that they make sense, so they are followed with:

What just happened?

This heading explains the working of tasks or instructions that you have just completed.

You will also find some other learning aids in the book, including:

Pop quiz – heading

These are short multiple-choice questions intended to help you test your own understanding.

Have a go hero – heading

These practical challenges give you ideas for experimenting with what you have learned.

You will also find a number of styles of text that distinguish between different kinds of information. Here are some examples of these styles, and an explanation of their meaning.

Code words in text are shown as follows: "The `fadeIn()` and `fadeOut()` methods perform the least complex animations available via jQuery"

A block of code is set as follows:

```
$("#next").click(function(event) {
  activeSlide++;
  rotate();
  event.preventDefault();
});
```

When we wish to draw your attention to a particular part of a code block, the relevant lines or items are set in bold:

```
$("#slider, #prev, #next").hover(function() {
  clearInterval(timer);
  pause = true;
}, function() {
  timer = setInterval(rotate, speed);
  pause = false;
});
```

New terms and **important words** are shown in bold. Words that you see on the screen, in menus or dialog boxes for example, appear in the text like this: "In this case, we clear the whole canvas, removing the space ship and any surviving aliens, and print the text **GAME OVER!** to the center of the canvas.".

Warnings or important notes appear in a box like this.

Tips and tricks appear like this.

Reader feedback

Feedback from our readers is always welcome. Let us know what you think about this book—what you liked or may have disliked. Reader feedback is important for us to develop titles that you really get the most out of.

To send us general feedback, simply send an e-mail to feedback@packtpub.com, and mention the book title through the subject of your message.

If there is a topic that you have expertise in and you are interested in either writing or contributing to a book, see our author guide on www.packtpub.com/authors.

Customer support

Now that you are the proud owner of a Packt book, we have a number of things to help you to get the most from your purchase.

Downloading the example code

You can download the example code files for all Packt books you have purchased from your account at http://www.packtpub.com. If you purchased this book elsewhere, you can visit http://www.packtpub.com/support and register to have the files e-mailed directly to you.

Errata

Although we have taken every care to ensure the accuracy of our content, mistakes do happen. If you find a mistake in one of our books—maybe a mistake in the text or the code—we would be grateful if you would report this to us. By doing so, you can save other readers from frustration and help us improve subsequent versions of this book. If you find any errata, please report them by visiting http://www.packtpub.com/submit-errata, selecting your book, clicking on the **errata submission form** link, and entering the details of your errata. Once your errata are verified, your submission will be accepted and the errata will be uploaded to our website, or added to any list of existing errata, under the Errata section of that title.

Piracy

Piracy of copyright material on the Internet is an ongoing problem across all media. At Packt, we take the protection of our copyright and licenses very seriously. If you come across any illegal copies of our works, in any form, on the Internet, please provide us with the location address or website name immediately so that we can pursue a remedy.

Please contact us at copyright@packtpub.com with a link to the suspected pirated material.

We appreciate your help in protecting our authors, and our ability to bring you valuable content.

Questions

You can contact us at questions@packtpub.com if you are having a problem with any aspect of the book, and we will do our best to address it.

1

Getting Started

Welcome to the jQuery 2.0 Animation Techniques Beginner's Guide. Over the course of the book we'll look at each and every method that produces or controls animations available in the jQuery JavaScript library. We'll see how the methods are used, the arguments they are able to accept, and the different behavior they produce. We'll also look at how to use a range of accompanying resources, including selected jQuery plugins and the jQuery UI library.

In this introductory chapter, we'll look at the following topics:

- A brief history of animation on the Web
- Why animating your UIs is important
- Animation methods provided by jQuery
- The template file used by each of the examples
- A basic animation example

Animation on the Web

In 1989, CompuServe released GIF89a, an enhanced version of the popular GIF image format, which allowed a sequence of frames to be stored as a single image and played by supporting software.

The GIF format was already popular on what passed for the Internet in those days (remember, the World Wide Web didn't even exist until 1991) due to its small file size, lossless compression, and wide support. The enhanced version which allowed animations that anyone could create themselves, provided they had supporting software, quickly became popular.

In addition to animated GIFs, browser vendors added support for proprietary HTML elements that handled animation natively, such as the `<blink>` and `<marquee>` elements, which added different animated effects to text.

Neither of these elements was particularly attractive or successful, and the W3C, as well as leading industry accessibility and usability experts advised against their use in most cases. Different browsers at that time supported one or the other of these elements, but not both. Both elements were added by their respective vendors as part of the original browser wars.

In the late 1990s, popular browsers added support for a technique known as **Dynamic HTML** (**DHTML**), which allowed scripting languages to modify the contents of a page after the page had loaded. DHTML wasn't any single technology, but rather a collection of techniques (JavaScript, CSS, DOM, and so on) that worked together to enable a basic level of interactivity and/or animation.

In fact, DHTML made it possible to create quite advanced animations, but restrictions in the early implementations of the required technologies, as well as hugely varying browser support made DHTML tricky at best.

This era also saw the release and the rise of Flash (and Shockwave, a competing technology that was eventually subsumed by Macromedia—which was later acquired by Adobe in 2005), a vector and raster graphics format that allowed audio and video streaming, frame-by-frame animation, and a host of other features. Flash quickly became popular, and at the time of writing is still the number one format for web-based video, browser-based gaming, and advertising.

Gradual standardization of the DOM across (most) browsers, as well as the rise of JavaScript libraries such as jQuery, which abstracted away the differences that remained between browsers, have opened up animation to a much wider range of people than ever before. The term DHTML isn't often used these days because of its connotations with poor support between browsers, but the underlying principles and techniques that drive many interactive and animated sites remain similar.

Today, in addition to the animations made plausible and accessible by JavaScript libraries, we have much newer and much more exciting possibilities with CSS3 and native HTML elements such as the `<canvas>` element, which provides complete pixel-level control over an area of the page. We'll be looking at some CSS3 animation techniques, as well as the `<canvas>` element in more detail towards the end of the book. Flash-based animation is on the decline for the first time this century, and new technologies are poised on the horizon.

The power of animated UIs

Modern operating systems use animations constantly to engage their users and to create a more compelling computing experience. When used in the right way, animations provide assistance to the users of the system, to lead and guide them through different tasks, provide context or feedback, and reinforce positive actions.

A good example of this is the way that applications are minimized in Windows 7 or OS X—the application appears to squish down into the icon on the taskbar/dock, which shows the user where to go when they want to return to the application. It's the simple details like this that can be most effective.

Good animations can lend an air of sleek professionalism to an interface and make it appear more advanced or more modern. Apple's iPhone (or iPad) is a perfect example— the seamless use of subtle animations and transitions within the operating system and its applications allow the user to connect with the device in a profoundly satisfying and immersive way. Anything that appears or disappears is faded smoothly in or out, and menus and content panels slide in or out from the top or the sides. Sudden events can unsettle or distract users, but a well-timed animation can help to make them aware that something is happening or something is about to happen.

Be warned though, badly executed, clumsy, or overly pointless animations can do the opposite, making your interface appear basic, poorly designed, or inferior. No animation can be better than poor animation. Even if your application works perfectly, superfluous animations can leave your users feeling frustrated and cause them to forgo your application or website.

Desktop computers and a rapidly growing number of mobile and handheld devices are easily powerful enough to handle quite complex animations, and with integrated hardware acceleration and more refined CSS3 and HTML5 making its way into the latest browsers, the possibilities of what can be achieved on the Web are increasing exponentially.

When to use animations

Animations can make a great impression and enhance the user experience in the following situations:

- When showing or hiding windows, pop ups, and content panels
- When something is moved to a different area of the window or page
- When something has changed state on the page as a result of the action of the user
- To lead the user to a specific call to action or bring their attention to something important

When not to use animations

Too many animations in unnecessary places can be damaging. Try and avoid animations, or at least give them serious consideration, in the following situations:

◆ When an action needs to be repeated very frequently by the user

◆ Where the devices known to use the system are likely to be incapable of displaying the animation adequately

◆ On time-sensitive actions or processes

 Bear in mind that these are guidelines only, not laws which must be obeyed at all costs, and they are certainly not definitive. There are few situations where animations should never, ever be used and few situations where they must always be used.

Use your judgment to determine whether an animation is suitable for your application or page and its intended audience. If possible, give your users the chance to enable or disable animations based on their own personal preferences.

Animation checklist

Before implementing an animation in our pages or applications, consider the following checklist of questions:

◆ Is the animation appropriate for your target users?

◆ Is the animation practical?

◆ Does the animation add value or enhance the user experience?

◆ Will the animation run at appropriate speeds on the devices that are most likely to be used?

If you can answer yes to all of the above questions, the animation will probably be a positive feature. If you answered no to any of these questions, you probably need to stop and think about what you are trying to achieve by adding the animation, and whether or not it could be better achieved in some other manner.

Animating with jQuery

jQuery (http://jquery.com) provides a range of animation methods natively, without the use of additional effect libraries or plugins. There are, however, many plugins contributed from the online community, including jQuery UI (http://jqueryui.com), the official UI library for jQuery, which extends jQuery's animation capabilities. Natively, jQuery provides methods that add sliding and fading behavior with minimal configuration and which work cross-browser. It also exposes methods related to managing the animation queue, and provides a means for creating custom animations that work on almost all numerical CSS styles. Over the course of this book, we'll look at every animation method that the library contains in detail. These methods are listed here with descriptions of each:

Methods	Description
animate()	It performs a custom animation of a set of CSS properties.
clearQueue()	It removes from the queue all items that have not yet been run.
delay()	It sets a timer to delay execution of subsequent items in the queue.
dequeue()	It executes the next function on the queue for the matched elements.
fadeIn()	It displays the matched elements by fading them to opaque.
fadeOut()	It hides the matched elements by fading them to transparent.
fadeTo()	It adjusts the opacity of the matched elements.
fadeToggle()	It displays or hides the matched elements by animating their opacity.
finish()	It stops the currently-running animation, removes all of the queued animations, and completes all of the animations for the matched elements.
hide()	It hides the matched elements.
queue()	It shows the queue of functions to be executed on the matched elements.
show()	It displays the matched elements.
slideDown()	It displays the matched elements with a sliding motion.
slideToggle()	It displays or hides the matched elements with a sliding motion.
slideUp()	It hides the matched elements with a sliding motion.
stop()	It stops the currently-running animation on the matched elements.
toggle()	It displays or hides the matched elements.

It's important to note that there are two properties that can change the Global jQuery Object. These are listed below:

Property	Description
`jQuery.fx.interval`	It is the rate (in milliseconds) at which animations fire.
`jQuery.fx.off`	It globally disables all animations.

All in all, it gives us a powerful and robust environment to easily add almost any type of animation that we can conceive.

Animation is also a popular theme for plugins, with many available plugins that bring different types of animations to our fingertips for instant implementation with minimal configuration. We'll look at several plugins later in the book.

Creating the project folder

So, that's the template file that we'll be referring to and using in the code examples throughout the book. Let's also take a moment to look at the folder structure that the example files use. Create a project folder and call it `jquery-animation` or any similar name. Within this, create three new folders and call them `css`, `img`, and `js`.

The HTML pages we create will go into the `jquery-animation` folder alongside the subfolders. All of the CSS files we create will go into the `css` folder, and all of the images that we use in the examples will go into the `img` folder. The jQuery library and any additional script files we use or create will go into the `js` folder. This is also the directory structure you'll find if you download and unpack the accompanying code archive containing all of the examples.

The template file

Each of the example files we'll create throughout the course of this book will rely on a common set of elements. Rather than repeatedly showing these same elements in every single code section and examples in the book, we'll take a look at them just once here:

```
<!DOCTYPE html>
<html lang="en">
  <head>
    <meta charset="utf-8">
    <title></title>
    <link rel="stylesheet" href="css/.css">
  </head>
  <body>
```

```
<script src="js/jquery.js"></script>
<script>
    $(function(){

    });
</script>
</body>
</html>
```

Downloading the example code

You can download the example code files for all Packt books you have purchased from your account at http://packtpub.com. If you purchased this book elsewhere, you can visit http://packtpub.com/support and register to have the files e-mailed directly to you.

Save a copy of this file into the jquery-animation folder we just created and call it template.html. This is the base file that we'll use for every single example, so when we start working through the examples and I say *add the following markup to the* <body> *of the template file*, it means insert it directly between the opening <body> tag and the first <script> tag in the template file we just created in the preceding code. Whenever we add any JavaScript to the template file, it will be added within the anonymous function in the second <script> tag.

Let's take a look at what the template file contains. We start out with the HTML5 doctype declaration, as we'll be using plenty of HTML5 elements in our examples. We also set the lang attribute of the <html> element to en and the <meta> tag's charset attribute to utf-8, neither of which are strictly required, but are nevertheless best practice.

Next comes an empty <title> element, to which we can add the name of each example and a <link> element with an incomplete href, ready for us to add the name of the stylesheet that each example will use.

Since the versions prior to **Internet Explorer 9** (**IE9**) don't support any HTML5 elements, we need to use Remy Sharp's html5shiv script to make this browser use HTML5 correctly. We can link to the online version of this file for convenience using a conditional comment that targets all of the versions of IE lower than version 9. Feel free to download html5.js and store it locally if you plan on playing with the examples in IE while disconnected from the Internet.

To get the most out of the examples throughout the book, it would probably be wise to upgrade to the latest stable release versions of the most common browsers, which at the time of writing are *Firefox 24*, *Chrome 30*, *Safari 6*, and *Opera 17* (although expect these to change quite rapidly).

It's important to note that jQuery 2.0 doesn't support *oldIE*, meaning IE8 and below. For this reason, we won't be covering any browser compatibility fixes for those versions of IE.

If your project needs to be compatible with IE8 or older, you'll need to use **jQuery 1.10** or below. Furthermore, if your project uses HTML5 elements and needs to be compatible with IE8 or below, you'll need to use `html5shiv` (`https://code.google.com/p/html5shiv`).

IE9 does support a lot of HTML5 and CSS3, so using the `html5shiv` file in general will only be required as long as IE8 holds its top spot as the world's most used browser. At the time of writing, Internet Explorer 8 had a market share of 21 percent worldwide according to NetMarketShare (`http://netmarketshare.com`). With 19 percent, IE10 comes in second and Chrome 29, FireFox 23 and IE9 are following shortly behind. The `<body>` tag of the page is empty, except for some `<script>` tags. We'll obviously use jQuery in every example, so the first tag links to that. The current version of jQuery is 2.0 at the time of writing (but like the browser versions, this is likely to change pretty quickly).

Throughout the book, we'll be using a local version of jQuery, so that we won't have to rely on being connected to the Internet or worry about Internet slowness. However, in most cases, in production, it's recommended to link to one of the 4 CDNs (Content Delivery Network) for jQuery. These can be found below:

CDN hosted by	URL
jQuery	`http://code.jquery.com`
Google	`https://developers.google.com/speed/libraries/devguide?csw=1#jquery`
Microsoft	`http://asp.net/ajaxlibrary/cdn.ashx#jQuery_Releases_on_the_CDN_0`
CDNJS	`http://cdnjs.com/libraries/jquery`

In the second `<script>` tag we have an empty function, into which all of the example JavaScript code we write will go. We pass the jQuery object into our anonymous function and alias it to the `$` character. Although not strictly necessary (except in the example where we create a jQuery plugin), this is another good habit to get into.

A basic animation example

Let's look at a basic example of the kind of animation that can help reassure our visitors that something is happening. If the user performs an action, and the result is not displayed immediately, providing feedback to the user that their action is in the process of being executed is a helpful use of animation.

In the next screenshot we can see the loading indicator centered beneath the **Initiate the action** button. It features three separate loading bars which sequentially light up to show that something is happening. Each bar is styled slightly differently.

Time for action – creating an animated loader

In this example we'll create a simple animated loading indicator that we can start when a particular process is initiated and stop once the process has completed.

1. Open up the template file that we just looked at and add the following `<button>` element to `<body>` (this should go before the `<script>` elements):

```
<button id="go">Initiate the action</button>
```

2. Next, in the empty function in the second `<script>` element at the bottom of the page, add the following code:

```
var loader = $("<div></div>", {
  id: "loader"
}).css("display", "none");
var bar = $("<span></span>").css("opacity", 0.2);
var loadingInterval = null;
for (var x = 0; x < 3; x++) {
  bar.clone().addClass("bar-" + x).appendTo(loader);
}
loader.insertAfter("#go");

function runLoader() {
  var firstBar = loader.children(":first"),
  secondBar = loader.children().eq(1),
  thirdBar = loader.children(":last");

  firstBar.fadeTo("fast", 1, function () {
    firstBar.fadeTo("fast", 0.2, function () {
      secondBar.fadeTo("fast", 1, function () {
```

```
        secondBar.fadeTo("fast", 0.2, function () {
          thirdBar.fadeTo("fast", 1, function () {
            thirdBar.fadeTo("fast", 0.2);
          });
        });
      });
    });
  });
};

$("#go").click(function () {
if (!$("#loader").is(":visible") ) {
  loader.show();
  loadingInterval = setInterval(function () {
    runLoader();
  }, 1200);
} else {
  loader.hide();
  clearInterval(loadingInterval);
}
});
```

3. Save the file as loading.html in the main project folder (jquery-animation).
    Finally, we'll need to add a few basic styles to the example. Create a new file in your
    text editor and add the following code to it:

```
#loader { margin:10px 0 0 36px; }
#loader span {
  display:block;
  width:6px;
  float:left;
  margin-right:6px;
  border:1px solid #336633;
  position:relative;
  background-color:#ccffcc;
}
#loader .bar-0 {
  height:15px;
  bottom:-20px;
}
#loader .bar-1 {
  height:25px;
  bottom:-10px;
}
#loader .bar-2 {
  height:35px;
  margin-right:0;
}
```

4. Save this file in the css folder as `loading.css` and update the HTML file to call this stylesheet.

5. At this point, your code should look like the following screenshot once we click on the button:

What just happened?

The `<button>` hardcoded onto the page is used to show and hide the loading animation. This is done purely for the purpose of this example. In an actual implementation, we'd show the loading animation at the start of a load operation, when new content is being added to the page for example, and then hide it again once the operation is complete.

The first thing we did inside the outer function is set some variables. We created a new `<div>` element as a container for the loader, using an **object literal** as the second argument in the anonymous function to give it an `id` of `loader`. We then set its style to `display:none` with jQuery's `css()` method so that it is not immediately visible.

 An *object* literal is a list of paired values separated by commas and wrapped in curly braces.

We also created a new `<span>` element, which will be used as a template to create the three individual loading bars. We set its opacity to `0.2` (20% opaque) using the `css()` method. jQuery normalizes this style for us so that it works correctly in Internet Explorer. The last variable, `loadingInterval`, will be used to store `id` of an **interval** so that we can clear the interval when we need to. We set this to null initially, as the interval has not yet been set.

 An *interval* is a numerical value set (in milliseconds) to pause or delay an action.

Once our variables have been defined and initialized, we then execute a short `for` loop, with just three iterations. Within this loop, we clone the span element we created, give it a class name (so that each bar can be styled separately), and then append it to the container. Once the three loading bars have been added to the container, we insert the loader after the `<button>` element.

Next, we define a function called `runLoader`. This is the function that will be repeatedly called by the interval. The function doesn't run until the button is clicked. Within this function, we cache the selector for each of the three individual bars and then run a series of nested functions.

We first increased the first-loading bar to full opacity using the `fadeTo()` jQuery animation method. This method takes a string indicating the speed of the animation as its first argument (in milliseconds, or using strings `"fast"` or `"slow"`), the opacity that the element should be faded to as its second argument (values range from 0-1, including decimals such as 0.50), and a callback function as the third argument. The callback function is executed as soon as the animation ends.

In the callback function, we then fade the first loading bar back to its original opacity of `0.2`. We supply another callback function to this method call, and within this callback function we animate the second loading bar to full opacity and then back to its original opacity. The same process is repeated for the third loading bar.

Finally, we use the jQuery `click()` method to add two functions which will be executed alternately each time the button is clicked. We'll use an `if` statement to check whether our `#loader` element is visible on the page by using `.is(":visible")` and adding an exclamation point (`!`) so that it returns true if the `#loader` element is not visible. If it isn't visible, we'll show the loader and then set the interval that repeatedly calls the `runLoader()` function. If the element is already visible, we hide the loader and clear the interval.

Have a go hero – extending the loading animation

I mentioned that we could use the loading animation when making requests and waiting for a response. Try using it with jQuery's AJAX methods, showing the loader just before making the request, and hiding it again once the response has been processed. The JSONP example, which retrieves images of cats, on the jQuery website (`http://api.jquery.com/jQuery.getJSON`), makes a great test case. Depending on the speed of your connection, the loader may not be visible for very long.

Pop quiz – basic animation with jQuery

Q1. Thinking about what we discussed earlier regarding when and when not to use animations, when would be an appropriate time to use this animation?

1. When there is a browser-intensive operation taking place

2. When there is a delay between something being requested from the server and the request returning from the server, but where the processing required by the browser is minimal

3. As an alternative to a Flash animation

4. When animated GIF images are not supported

Q2. What arguments are used with jQuery's `fadeTo()` method?

1. An integer representing the ending opacity

2. An object containing configuration options for the animation

3. A string or integer representing the speed or duration of the animation as the first argument, the ending opacity of the target element, and optionally a callback function to be executed when the animation ends

4. No arguments are required

Summary

In this introductory chapter, we looked at a brief history of animation on the Web including how it began, early HTML elements and browser support, the rise of Flash, and the direction it's heading in the not-too-distant future.

We also looked at how animations can be used in a user interface to enhance the user experience. We saw some guidelines as to when animation should and shouldn't be used and looked at some of the things we should consider when implementing animations.

We concluded the chapter with a basic example of using a loading animation. In this example, we used the `fadeTo()` jQuery method to change the opacity of elements on the page and a simple interval to play the animation. We didn't cover the method in full detail but we saw one example of how it can be used. We'll look at this method in more detail in the next chapter, which covers all of the fading animations provided by jQuery.

In the next chapter, we'll be focusing on animating images. We'll be creating a basic image rotator, and then extending the functionality of that script to build more functionality on top. We'll be left with a very lightweight image rotator that we can use on future development projects.

2
Image Animation

In this chapter we'll be creating a basic image rotator (slider) using jQuery animation functions. We'll also be extending the functionality of our script to pause the animation when our users hover over the rotator. Then we'll be adding previous and next links to the script to allow users the ability to scroll through our images at their own pace. Lastly, we'll be adding in a pagination link, so that our user can page through the images in our image rotator.

Image animation

On your journey through the world of jQuery, you'll find that some form of content or image rotation is necessary at times. Image rotators are a more visually appealing way to display sets of images than having them displayed straight down the page. They can also lead to a more compact and efficient design, allow for preloading of content or images, and also can give us the ability to control what and when the user sees.

 Image rotators are often referred to as a **slideshow**, **slider**, **scroller**, or **carousel**, based on the varying functionality.

We'll be talking about the following animation methods in this chapter:

- `fadeIn()`
- `fadeOut()`
- `fadeToggle()`

Fading animations

The `fadeIn()` and `fadeOut()` methods perform the least complex animations available via jQuery. They simply adjust the opacity of selected elements to either show or hide the element and can be used with no additional configuration. The `fadeToggle()` method is almost as simple, but does provide some basic logic to check the selected element's current state.

Elements that are hidden with `display:none` will be set to their correct display type (either `display:block` for block-level elements or `display:inline` for inline elements) where possible at the start of a `fadeIn()` animation. It is important to note this as your CSS styles might impact the appearance of an element that you are fading in. An element's natural display type is used wherever possible, so hidden `<li>` elements are set to `display:list-item`, and hidden `<td>` elements are set to `display:table-cell`.

Elements that are set to `display:block` (or are set to another display type but nevertheless visible on the page) will be set to `display:none` at the end of a `fadeOut()` animation. Elements will switch between their visible and non-visible states when the `fadeToggle()` method is used.

Elements that are to be shown using the `fadeIn()` method must be initially hidden with `display:none` while the elements that are hidden with `visibility:hidden` for example, will remain hidden at the end of the animation because the fade methods specifically alter the `opacity` and `display` property, and not the `visibility` property.

In their simplest forms, these methods can be used without any additional configuration. We can simply call the methods on any collection of selected elements without using any arguments:

- `$(elements).fadeIn();`
- `$(elements).fadeOut();`
- `$(elements).fadeToggle();`

When no arguments are provided, the animations will have the default duration of 400 milliseconds and the default easing of `swing`. We'll talk about animation easing very shortly.

Configuring the animations with arguments

With arguments, the fading methods may take the following form (square brackets denote optional arguments):

```
$(elements).fadeIn([duration] [,easing] [,callback]);
$(elements).fadeOut([duration] [,easing] [,callback]);
$(elements).fadeToggle([duration] [,easing] [,callback]);
```

We can control the duration of the animation using the `duration` argument to specify either an integer in milliseconds or strings `"slow"`, and `"fast"`. These strings are shortcuts for 600 and 200 milliseconds respectively. The default duration given if one isn't specified is 400.

We can also supply 0 as the `duration` argument, which will effectively disable the animation. It's unlikely that we'd need to do this as it would be more efficient to not use an animation at all, but it is useful to know. I should point out that the fade will still occur; it will just happen over a duration of 0 milliseconds. Doing this would be the same as using `.hide()`, essentially.

The easing argument can be changed from its default value of `swing` to `linear`, which causes the animation to progress at the same speed throughout the animation. The default, `swing`, causes the animation to start slowly, speed up slightly, and then slow down towards the end of the animation.

The `duration` argument relates to the length of time the animation takes to run and not the speed of the animation. Therefore, a higher value will mean a slower, longer animation and not a faster, shorter animation. The number of easing types can be greatly increased using plugins. We'll look at the extra easing types added by jQuery UI later in the book.

We may supply a **callback** function (either a function reference or an anonymous function, with the latter being more commonplace). This callback function will be executed after the animation ends for each element in the selection, so it may be triggered more than once if more than a single element is being animated.

A callback function is a function that is passed inside another function as a parameter.

The following example of callback code triggers an alert once the animation is complete (callback in bold):

```
$(".selector").fadeOut("slow", function() {
   alert("callback triggered!"); });
```

You'll often see the preceding line formatted like the following block of code for readability:

```
$(".selector").fadeOut("slow", function() {
   alert("callback triggered!");
});
```

Time for action – setting up the markup and styling

To begin with, we need to create the elements that will be used in the example and the styling to set their visual appearance.

1. Create a new HTML document using the template file we created in *Chapter 1, Getting Started*, and in between the `<body>` tag add the following underlying markup for our image slider:

```
<div class="container">
  <div id="slider">
    <img src="http://placekitten.com/200/200?image=1">
    <img src="http://placekitten.com/200/200?image=2">
    <img src="http://placekitten.com/200/200?image=3">
    <img src="http://placekitten.com/200/200?image=4">
    <img src="http://placekitten.com/200/200?image=5">
    <img src="http://placekitten.com/200/200?image=6">
    <img src="http://placekitten.com/200/200?image=7">
  </div>
</div>
```

2. Save the page in the `jquery-animation` directory as `image-rotator.html`.

3. We'll also need to add in our stylesheet for this example. In the HTML file we just created, add `image-rotator` to our placeholder stylesheet link.

4. Next we should create the stylesheet we just linked to. In a new file, add the following code:

```
.container {
  position:relative;
  width:200px;
  height:200px;
}
#slider img {
  position:absolute;
  display:none;
  border-radius:3px;
}
```

5. Save this file as `image-rotator.css` in the `css` folder within our project folder.

What just happened?

For this example, we'll be using seven images in our image rotator. This can easily be changed based on our needs by simply adding additional images to `<div id="slider">`.

We wrapped our `#slider` element in a `<div>` element with a class of `container` so that we can set the dimensions of our image rotator in case all our images aren't of the same width and height. Also, we set `position:relative` to the `#slider` div so that the rotator images being set to `position:absolute` don't get removed from the page flow.

> When an element is set to `position:absolute`, the element no longer holds open the space that it's placed in, which allows other elements behind or in front of it, based on the other CSS used on the surrounding elements. This is similar to what happens when an element is floated and it's removed from the page flow.
>
> It's important to note that in some cases if an element (or group of elements) are set to `position:absolute` without a parent element being set to `position:relative`, the `position:absolute` elements could come out of their parent element, which would collapse the parent element.

The images are set to `position:absolute` because they need to stack behind each other so that our image rotator element doesn't jump around as the images are being faded in and out. This is needed because all of the images will occupy the same relative position on the page. However, we only want 1 image to display at a time. Using `display:none` will turn off the visibility on all our images. This is needed so that we don't have to worry about the **stacking order** of our images. We want a good presentation on our images so we added a small `border-radius` on the images to soften the corners.

> **Stack order** refers to the order in which elements are stacked on a page. If an element is loaded before another element, it will be before the following element. The stack order can be modified in CSS using `z-index`, and by adding `position` to an element.

Pop quiz – using fadeIn()

Q1. Which strings can be passed into the `fadeIn()` method as the first argument?

1. The strings `"short"` or `"long"`, which refer to the duration of the animation.

2. The strings `"low"` or `"high"`, which refer to the opacity that the element is faded to.

3. The strings `"slow"` or `"fast"`, which refer to the duration of the animation.

4. A hexadecimal string specifying `background-color` of the element

Q2. What else can be passed into the method?

1. A string specifying the easing function to use for the animation, and a callback function to be executed once the animation ends.
2. An object containing additional configuration options.
3. An array containing additional configuration options.
4. A callback function to be executed at the start of an animation, and a callback function to be executed at the end of the animation.

Scripting the image slider

Next, we're going to add the finishing touches to our image rotator by adding the jQuery code that'll animate our images.

Time for action – scripting the image rotator

Now let's add the code for the script that will animate our images. Add the following code inside the anonymous function below the `<body>` tag:

```
var image = $("#slider img");
var numSlides = image.length;
var activeSlide = 0;
var speed = 2000;
var fade = 1000;
var timer = setInterval(rotate, speed);
image.eq(activeSlide).show();

function rotate() {
  activeSlide++;

  if (activeSlide == numSlides) {
    activeSlide = 0;
  }

  image.not(activeSlide).fadeOut(fade);
  image.eq(activeSlide).fadeIn(fade);
}
```

What just happened?

The first thing we did was we cached a reference to all the `<img>` elements located inside the `#slider` element. We'll be referencing it several times, so it is more efficient to only select it from the **Document Object Model (DOM)** once. For performance reasons, it is generally best to minimize the number of DOM operations that are carried out.

For counting the number of images we used `length()`. This counts the number of child elements (`<img>`) inside the parent element (`#slider`). For our example, we used seven images. Using the `length()` function to count the number of `<img>` elements, we can easily add or remove images from the image slider without altering the jQuery code.

Our `activeSlide` variable is set to 0 so that we start with the first image in our set. This is generally something you won't want to change unless you want to start on a specific image. This number can be changed to any number you like, as long as we have at least that number of images in our set of images.

The `activeSlide` variable represents the position within the group of elements we just selected. The `length()` function returns the number of elements, starting from 0. In our example, `image.length()` will return 6 and therefore `activeSlide` can be 0 to 6 since there are seven `<img>` elements. We initialize `activeSlide` to 0, so we start at the first image in the sequence. If we want to start on a different image, initialize `activeSlide` to that position within the group keeping in mind that the first position is 0 and not 1.

To set the time between each execution of the `rotate()` function, we set the `speed` variable to 2000 milliseconds (2 seconds). 2 seconds is a good speed for our example but you'll want to set it to a longer duration depending on the images that you're rotating. If you have text on your images that you want your users to read, you should set the rotation speed based on how long you think it will take your users to comfortably read all the text. If you have images with high detail in them, set the speed to something you think is a generous amount of time to take in all the detail. In case you have a clickable element that requires a "call to action", this time will need to be taken into consideration based on how long it takes the user to digest the information and take the action you want them to take.

Our `fade` variable is set to 1000 (1 second) as this is a decent speed for fading out the images. This can be changed to fit your needs and you'll find that there is no standard time for it or the speed. You'll need to tailor these times to give your users the best possible experience on your website.

The `setInterval()` (native JavaScript method) function creates a timer within the script which executes the function that's called every interval. In our example, `setInterval()` will execute the `rotate()` function, but wait to call it again until the amount of time specified in the `speed` variable has passed. Since `speed` is set to 2000, the `rotate()` function will be executed every 2 seconds.

> With arguments, the `setInterval` event may take the following form:
> `setInterval(function, duration);`

We then tell the script to display the active image using `show()`. Since we set the `activeSlide` variable to 0 initially, the first image in our set will be displayed first. This is needed because if you recall, in our CSS we're turning off the visibility of all of the images in our rotator using `display:none`. If you change the initial value of the `activeSlide` variable, then that image will be the first one to be shown when the script starts.

Next, we move on to the meat of our script. For our vegetarian readers, whatever protein equivalent you eat in your diet, Soy? Tofu? Anyway, the `rotate()` function is where we do most of the heavy lifting in our code. The code above the `rotate()` function is mostly the settings for our image rotator to use. Inside our beefy `rotate()` function we have a variable (`activeSlide`) that we're incrementing by one each time it is called. This is needed to set our active image to the next image in our set each time the function loops.

The `if` statement is used to reset the `activeSlide` number back to 0 once the script has reached the last `<img>` element in the selected group.

Finally, we have the two most important lines in our code (arguably). We're using the `fadeOut()` animation function for all images that is `not()` our active image. Then we're using `fadeIn()` for the image that is equal to the `activeSlide` image. You'll notice the variable fade inside our `fadeOut()` and `fadeIn()` animations. This determines the speed at which the animation is performed. Along with some other jQuery animation functions, `"slow"` and `"fast"` can also be used—which is 600 and 200 milliseconds respectively.

This is a screenshot of what we just created using the previous code. You'll notice how the first image fades out at the same time our next image fades in. This effect is called **cross-fading**.

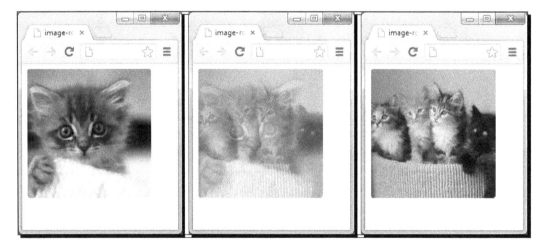

Pop quiz – length() and milliseconds

Q1. What does `length()` refer to?

1. The character count of a variable.
2. The number of elements in the object.
3. The width of the object.
4. The amount of time an animation should run for.

Q2. How many milliseconds are there in 1 second?

1. 10
2. 100
3. 1000
4. 10000

Time for action – extending the pause-on-hover functionality

Pause-on-hover is necessary when your images have a lot of detail, text that your users need to read, or have a specific call to action that you want them to make. Even if you don't have need of any of those things, it's still a good idea to add this functionality as it allows the user to get a good look at the images if they wish.

The following screenshot illustrates that the image rotation has stopped when the user hovered over the image:

To detect when we hover on and off our image rotator so that we can pause our image rotator, we need to add the following code to the line below `image.eq(activeSlide).show();`:

```
$("#slider").hover(function() {
  clearInterval(timer);
}, function() {
  timer = setInterval(rotate, speed);
});
```

What just happened?

We added a hover event to gain the ability to tell our script when we're hovering over the #slider element and when we've moved away from the element. We're using clearInterval() (native JavaScript method) on the timer variable to stop the timer on our rotator, effectively pausing the animation.

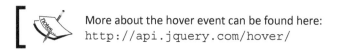 More about the hover event can be found here: http://api.jquery.com/hover/

It's important to note that stop() and clearQueue() are other methods to stop an animation or function from running. However, in this example, we don't want to use them because they stop our animations immediately. That can mean it will pause an animation halfway through and will display both (the current active and the next active) images partially faded on top of each other. Alternatively, we could have left the interval running and used a flag in the rotate() function to determine whether to perform the fadeIn() or fadeOut() methods.

The next line tells the script that we are no longer hovering over it and to resume animating the images. The timer is then reset back to what we originally set it to at the beginning using setInterval (native JavaScript method).

Time for action – extending the previous and next link features

To give your users more controls over the speed of your rotating images, we're going to add next and previous links as shown in the following steps:

1. We need to add the anchor tags that will be used for our previous and next links. To do this, add the following code between the last two `</div>` tags:

```
<a id="prev">prev</a>
<a id="next">next</a>
```

2. Our next and previous links will need some basic styling, so let's add the following lines of CSS to the bottom of our `image-rotator.css` file:

```
#prev, #next {
  position:absolute;
  bottom:10px;
  padding:5px 10px;
  color:#000;
  background:#FFF;
  border-radius:3px;
  text-decoration:none;
  opacity:0.7;
}
#prev:hover, #next:hover {
  opacity:1;
  cursor:pointer;
}
#prev {left:10px;}
#next {right:10px;}
```

3. For handling the click events on the next and previous links, we'll need to add the following code right above the `rotate()` function:

```
$("#prev").click(function(event) {
  activeSlide--;
  rotate();
  event.preventDefault();
});

$("#next").click(function(event) {
  activeSlide++;
  rotate();
  event.preventDefault();
});
```

4. Add the following lines of code above `image.not(activeSlide).fadeOut(fade);`:

```
if (activeSlide < 0) {
  activeSlide = numSlides - 1;
}
```

5. Update the `rotate()` function by replacing `activeSlide++` with the following code:

```
if (!pause == true) {
  activeSlide++;
}
```

6. Find the `hover()` function and replace it with the following code (the new code is highlighted):

```
$("#slider, #prev, #next").hover(function() {
  clearInterval(timer);
  pause = true;
}, function() {
  timer = setInterval(rotate, speed);
  pause = false;
});
```

The following screenshot shows that, after the next link is clicked, our image rotator moves to the next image:

What just happened?

In the third step, we're adding in two click functions for the previous and next links. We are decrementing the active image number by one on the previous function and incrementing by one on the next function. Then we need to call the rotate function again so that our old image fades out and our new one fades in. We use `preventDefault()` (native JavaScript method) so that the previous and next links don't add a hashtag (#) to the URL in our address bar. This prevents the previous and next links from working like a traditional anchor tag.

The fourth step allows us to move backwards in our image set. This `if` statement is similar to the `if` statement we already have in our `rotate()` function used to reset the active variable if it's equal to the number of images in our rotator.

We need to change the `rotate()` function so it only increments the `active` image variable if our image rotator isn't being hovered over. To do this, we replaced the line that increments our `activeSlide` variable with an `if` statement. Using this `if` statement we're telling the script to only allow the `activeSlide` variable to increment if our user is not hovering over the image rotator.

We'll need to add in our next and previous links to the pause-on-hover function so that the image rotation will pause when you hover over those as well. This can be achieved by adding a comma after `#slider`, and adding in our `#next` and `#previous` ID selectors. We're setting the `pause` variable to a Boolean value of `true` or `false` based on whether or not we've triggered the `hover` event. This is needed to tell the `rotate` function to only increment the `activeSlide` variable if we are not hovering over it. To tell our script we are hovering over it, we're setting the variable `pause` to a value of `true`. Then we set it to `false` once our cursor leaves the image rotator.

Pop quiz – preventDefault() and setInterval()

Q1. What is `preventDefault()` used for?

1. Preventing the script from defaulting variables in the function.
2. Preventing the default action on an event it's used on.
3. Turning off all JavaScript errors in the function that it's used in.
4. Turning off JavaScript errors for variables that return a value of null.

Q2. What are the two arguments for the `setInterval()` method that need to be used?

1. `speed` and `time`
2. `function` and `duration`
3. `duration` and `speed`
4. `speed` and `function`

Time for action – extending the pagination functionality

To give our users even more control over our image rotator, we're going to add what's called **pagination**. Pagination allows you to move directly to a specific image in our rotator instead of having to click the next and previous links until we find the image we're looking for. This function is very helpful if we have a large number of images in our image rotator. To add pagination we perform the following steps:

Let's start by adding the following code to `image-rotator.css`:

```css
#pagination {
  position:absolute;
  top:10px;
  width:100%;
  text-align:center;
}
#pagination a {
  padding:2px 5px;
  color:#000;
  background:#FFF;
  border-radius:3px;
  text-decoration:none;
  opacity:0.7;
}
#pagination a:hover {
  opacity:1;
  cursor:pointer;
}
```

1. In `image-rotator.html`, add the following line directly under `var pause;`:

```
var paging = "";
```

2. In our HTML, we need to add the following code under `<a id="next" href="#">next</a>`:

```html
<div id="pagination"></div>
```

3. Place the following code below `image.eq(activeSlide).show();`:

```javascript
for (var page = 0; page < numSlides; page++) {
  paging += "<a rel=\"" + (page + 1) + "\">" + (page + 1) +
    "</a>\n";
}
$("#pagination").html(paging);
```

4. Find the `hover` event below and replace it with the following code (new code is highlighted):

```javascript
$("#slider, #prev, #next, #pagination").hover(function() {
  clearInterval(timer);
  pause = true;
}, function() {
  timer = setInterval(rotate, speed);
  pause = false;
});
```

5. Add the following code directly above our `rotate()` function:

```
$("#pagination a").click(function(event) {
  event.preventDefault();
  activeSlide = $(this).attr("rel") - 1;
  rotate();
});
```

The following screenshot illustrates the pagination feature we added, along with the fourth image displayed after clicking on the respective link:

What just happened?

The first thing we did was declare and set the new paging variable. Without this, we'll get nasty JavaScript errors in our code.

Using a `for` loop, we defined our page variable, telling it to continue looping until `page` is less than the number of images in our set and then increment that newly defined variable by one using `++`. The next line is the most complicated bit of code in our script so far, so stick with me! A variable followed by `+=` tells the variable to use what's already stored inside and to continue adding on to the end. This method of stringing together values or strings is called **concatenation**.

We then need to build the HTML structure of the pagination links. We're building a series of seven <a> tags, one for each image in our group. To print the image numbers on the links, we'll use (page + 1). We're using + 1 because JavaScript numbers things on what's called a **zero-index** or **zero-based numbering**, which means instead of starting at 1 when numbering a group or list of items, it starts with 0. This hasn't been a problem until now (because we weren't printing out the value), but we now need to tell our script to start at 1 so that it displays the pagination links properly. The last line of the for loop replaces the contents of #pagination and replaces it with the value stored inside the paging variable using html().

 The html() method is used to get or set the HTML contents on the selected element(s).

Again, we need to expand our pause-on-hover function to know to pause when we're hovering over our new #pagination element. If we don't do this, when you hover over the #pagination div, the images would continue to rotate.

We added another click function ($("#pagination a").click) to handle our pagination links. You'll notice the same preventDefault() we used before so that our links don't add the hashtag (#) to our page URL when clicking on the pagination links. The next line sets the activeSlide variable to the value of rel in our pagination anchor tag and then subtracts by one. This is done because we set it to increment by one to offset the zero-index problem we saw in the third step.

Finally, we added in the containing <div> element that'll hold all of our pagination links.

Have a Go Hero – extending the image rotator further

In this example, we used fadeIn() and fadeOut() to rotate our images. Have a go at extending the example so that the script can detect the child elements that should be animated.

Other ideas for extending the image rotator:

- Have the script to set the child element dimensions dynamically, allowing the script to scale to fit the content
- Building the ability to show more than one element at a time
- Giving the current active link in the pagination bar a different look so that our user knows which image the rotator is currently on
- Adding in additional transition effects (for example, slide)

Pop quiz – altering variables and zero index

Q1. What does using ++ after a variable do?

1. Merges the values of two variables together.

2. Tells the script to only allow adding to the variable and not subtracting.

3. Increments the variable by one.

4. Increments the variable by two.

Q2. What does **zero-index** mean?

1. That JavaScript counts starting with zero.

2. That a variable's default value is zero if not specifically defined.

3. A method in which an element's index is set to zero.

4. A method to set a variable's value to zero after being used.

Summary

In this chapter, we looked at some of jQuery's most basic animation methods. The fade methods are the simplest animation methods found in jQuery, only animating the opacity of the selected element(s).

The show(), hide(), and toggle() methods can also be used to perform animations but alter the dimensions of the element as well as its opacity. All of these methods are simple to use and require little or no additional configuration in order to run.

In the next chapter, we'll learn how to manipulate the background properties on elements to create background animations.

3
Background Animation

In the last chapter, we used the `fadeIn()` *and* `fadeOut()` *methods to animate image elements. In this chapter, we'll be using the* `animate()` *effect to animate the background color and learn how to animate the position of background images inside our elements. In Chapter 7, Custom Animation, we'll go further in depth as to everything that the* `animate()` *method is capable of.*

Background-color animation

Animating the background color of an element is a great way to draw our users' eyes to the object we want them to see. Another use for animating the background color of an element is to show that something has happened to the element. It's typically used in this way if the state of the object changes (added, moved, deleted, and so on), or if it requires attention to fix a problem. We'll learn about some of these things in the next two chapters.

 Due to the lack of support in jQuery 2.0 for animating background-color, we'll be using jQuery UI to give us the functionality we need to create this effect.

We'll be covering all of the beautiful things jQuery UI gives us the ability to do in *Chapter 6, Extending Animations with jQuery UI.*

Introducing the animate method

The `animate()` method is one of the most useful methods jQuery has to offer in its bag of tricks in the animation realm. With it, we're able to do things such as move an element across the page or alter and animate the properties of colors, backgrounds, text, fonts, the box model, position, display, lists, tables, generated content, and so on.

Time for action – animating the body background-color

Following the steps below, we're going to start by creating an example that changes the body background color.

1. Start by creating a new file (using our template) called `background-color.html` and save it in our `jquery-animation` folder.

2. Next, we'll need to include the jQuery UI library by adding this line directly under our jQuery library:

```
<script src="js/jquery-ui.min.js"></script>
```

A custom or stable build of jQuery UI can be downloaded from `http://jqueryui.com`, or you can link to the library using one of the three **Content Delivery Networks (CDNs)** below. For the fastest access to the library, go to `http://jqueryui.com`, scroll to the very bottom, and look for the **Quick Access** section. Using the jQuery UI library JS file there will work just fine for our need of the examples in this chapter.

Media Template: `http://code.jquery.com`

Google: `http://developers.google.com/speed/libraries/devguide#jquery-ui`

Microsoft: `http://asp.net/ajaxlibrary/cdn.ashx#jQuery_Releases_on_the_CDN_0`

CDNJS: `http://cdnjs.com/libraries/jquery`

3. Then, we'll add the following jQuery code to the anonymous function:

```
var speed = 1500;
$( "body" ).animate({ backgroundColor: "#D68A85" }, speed);
$( "body" ).animate({ backgroundColor: "#E7912D" }, speed);
$( "body" ).animate({ backgroundColor: "#CECC33" }, speed);
$( "body" ).animate({ backgroundColor: "#6FCD94" }, speed);
$( "body" ).animate({ backgroundColor: "#3AB6F1" }, speed);
$( "body" ).animate({ backgroundColor: "#8684D8" }, speed);
$( "body" ).animate({ backgroundColor: "#DD67AE" }, speed);
```

What just happened?

First, we added the jQuery UI library to our page. This was needed because of the lack of support for animating the background color in the current version of jQuery. Next, we added in the code that will animate our background. We then set the `speed` variable to `1500` (milliseconds) so that we can control the duration of our animation. Lastly, using the `animate()` method, we set the background color of the body element and set the duration to the variable we set above named `speed`. We duplicated the same line several times, changing only the hexadecimal value of the background color.

The following screenshot is an illustration of colors that the entire body background color animates through:

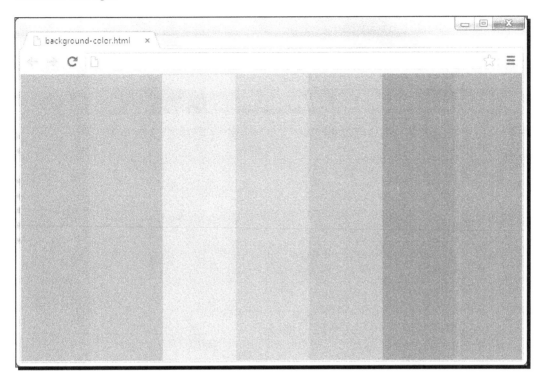

Chaining together jQuery methods

It's important to note that jQuery methods (`animate()`, in this case) can be chained together. Our code mentioned previously would look like the following if we chained the `animate()` methods together:

```
$("body")
    .animate({ backgroundColor: "#D68A85" }, speed)   //red
    .animate({ backgroundColor: "#E7912D" }, speed)   //orange
    .animate({ backgroundColor: "#CECC33" }, speed)   //yellow
    .animate({ backgroundColor: "#6FCD94" }, speed)   //green
    .animate({ backgroundColor: "#3AB6F1" }, speed)   //blue
    .animate({ backgroundColor: "#8684D8" }, speed)   //purple
    .animate({ backgroundColor: "#DD67AE" }, speed); //pink
```

Here's another example of chaining methods together:

```
$(selector).animate(properties).animate(properties)
.animate(properties);
```

Have a go hero – extending our script with a loop

In this example we used the `animate()` method and with some help from jQuery UI, we were able to animate the body background color of our page. Have a go at extending the script to use a loop, so that the colors continually animate without stopping once the script gets to the end of the function.

Pop quiz – chaining with the animate() method

Q1. Which code will properly animate our body background color from red to blue using chaining?

1. ```
   $("body")
       .animate({ background: "red" }, "fast")
       .animate({ background: "blue" }, "fast");
   ```

2. ```
   $("body")
       .animate({ background-color: "red" }, "slow")
       .animate({ background-color: "blue" }, "slow");
   ```

3. ```
   $("body")
       .animate({ backgroundColor: "red" })
       .animate({ backgroundColor: "blue" });
   ```

4. ```
   $("body")
       .animate({ backgroundColor, "red" }, "slow")
       .animate({ backgroundColor, "blue" }, "slow");
   ```

The illusion of depth with parallax

The term parallax, when used in the context of computer graphics, especially video games, refers to the technique of using multiple background layers that scroll at slightly different speeds to create the illusion of depth. Although not as widely deployed in modern gaming, thanks to the advent of richer 3D graphics engines, parallax is still seen frequently in portable gaming devices, and increasingly, on the Web.

A parallax effect is achievable using pure CSS, as demonstrated nicely on the Silverback site (see `http://silverbackapp.com` for the effect, and `http://blog.teamtreehouse.com/how-to-recreate-silverbacks-parallax-effect` for the details on how it was implemented). This application of parallax will only become apparent when the window is resized horizontally. While this is a fantastic effect when the window is resized, it doesn't help us if we want the effect to take more of a center stage.

Time for action – creating the stage and adding the styling

The underlying page requires just four elements (for this simple example), which sit in the `<body>` of the page.

1. Add the elements in the following structure to a fresh copy of the template file, between the `<body>` tag and the first `<script>` tag:

```
<div id="background"></div>
<div id="midground"></div>
<div id="foreground"></div>
<div id="ground"></div>
```

2. Save this page as `parallax-horizontal.html` in our `jquery-animation` folder.

3. The CSS in this example is equally as simple as the underlying HTML. Add the following code to a new file in your text editor:

```
div {
  width:100%;
  height:1000px;
  position:absolute;
  left:0;
  top:0;
}
#background { background:url(../images/background.png) repeat-x 0
  0; }
#midground { background:url(../images/midground.png) repeat-x 0 0;
  }
#foreground { background:url(../images/foreground.png) repeat-x 0
  0; }
#stage { background:url(../images/ground.png) repeat-x 0 100%; }
```

4. Save this file as `parallax- horizontal.css` in the `css` directory and update the HTML file we just created to link to this file.

5. At this point the page should look like the following screenshot:

The front area is the ground, the foreground layer is the darker colored bushes, the midground is the lighter colored bushes, and the background slice is the sky and clouds.

What just happened?

You'll also find the images for this example in the images folder of the code download accompanying this book. We have a separate image for each element that we wish to be part of the parallax effect, three in this example, one for the background, one for the midground, and one for the foreground.

The underlying HTML is also very simple. We just have a separate <div> for each layer of the background. In CSS, each image layer is positioned absolutely so that they overlay each other. Now, let's get the layers of the parallax moving!

Time for action – animating the background position

Now, for the <script> itself. At the bottom of the HTML file, as usual in the empty anonymous function, add the following code:

```
var bg = $("#background");
var mg = $("#midground");
var fg = $("#foreground");

$(document).keydown(function(e) {
  if (e.which === 39) { //right arrow key
    bg.animate({ backgroundPosition: "-=1px" }, 0, "linear" );
    mg.animate({ backgroundPosition: "-=10px" }, 0, "linear" );
    fg.animate({ backgroundPosition: "-=20px" }, 0, "linear" );
  }
});
```

If we run this page in a browser now, we should find that as we hold down the right arrow key, the different background image slices move at relatively slower speeds with the foreground almost rushing past and the background moving leisurely along.

What just happened?

In the script we first cache the selectors we'll be using so that we don't have to create a new jQuery object and select the elements from the DOM each time the background-position changes, which will be very frequently indeed. We then set a keydown event listener on the document object. Within the anonymous function we use as the event handler, we check whether the key code supplied by the which property of the event object (this is normalized by jQuery so it will be accessible via cross-browser) is equal to 39, which is the key code returned by the right arrow key.

We then call the `animate()` on `backgroundPosition` and we supplied relative values of `-=1px`, `-=10px`, and `-=20px` to move each layer at progressively faster speeds, which gives us the parallax effect. These animations are called simultaneously, and have their durations set to zero (0) milliseconds and `linear` easing. This is the last thing our `keydown` handler needs to do.

Have a go hero - extending parallax

In this example, the backgrounds animate only from right to left. Extend the example so that both the left to right and right to left motion is available. Need help getting started? You'll need to create another function for the left arrow key and increment the `backgroundPostion` values instead of decrementing like we did in our example.

Automatic background animation

In this example, we're going to make the background image animate up the page automatically, without any special interaction from our user.

Time for action – creating an automatic background animation

We're going to create an example that will automatically animate the background image now.

1. Create a new file using our template called `background-auto.html` and save it in our `jquery-animation` directory.

2. Since we only have one line of CSS for our example, we aren't going to create a stylesheet. We're going to drop it in the file we just created (`background-auto.html`) under the `<title>` tag:

```
<style>
  body {background:url(images/background.jpg) top center fixed;}
</style>
```

3. Next, we'll remove the stylesheet `<link>` since we won't be using it in this example. This will be the line directly after the code we just added.

4. Lastly, add the following code into our waiting anonymous function:

```
var yPos = 0;
var timer = setInterval(start, 50);

function start() {
    yPos = yPos - 5;
    $('body').css({ backgroundPosition: '50% ' + yPos + 'px'
      });
}
```

The following is a screenshot of what we just created. You'll notice that when viewing the example, the background image animates up the back from the bottom to the top.

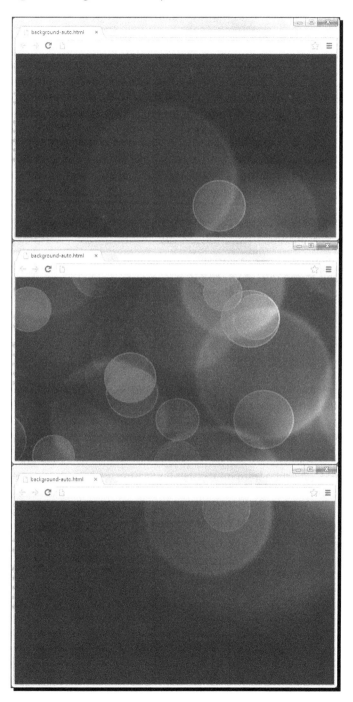

What just happened?

The first thing we did was declare our variable, yPos, as an integer. Doing this, as you may know, scares off any spooky JavaScript errors that haunt Internet Explorer and similarly, non-modern browser versions.

Next, we declared our timer variable using setInterval(). In the previous chapter, we learned that the parameters for this method are function and duration. Our function name is start, so we set the function parameter to that. We also set our duration to 50 (milliseconds), as this is a suitable time frame for our function to wait before executing again.

Then, we created a function that can be called by our timer named start. We take the current value of yPos and subtract it by five each time our function executes. The last line of our function is what does all of the heavy lifting. This line animates the <body> background image's position vertically five pixels each time the function comes to this line in our script.

Have a go hero – playing under the hood

Have a go at changing the timer duration and yPos offset values to see how these values affect the speed and frame rate at which our background animates. Another challenge would be to try to make the background animate horizontally instead of vertically, like we did for this example.

Let's make it diagonal!

Now, instead of making the background image animate vertically, we're going to animate it diagonally now. Hold on to your programming hats!

Time for action – animating the background diagonally

We're going to make our animation move diagonally now.

1. Let's use the same file as before (background-auto.html) and replace the code in our anonymous function with the code below (new code is highlighted):

```
var xPos = 0;
var yPos = 0;
var timer = setInterval(start, 50);

function start() {
    xPos = xPos - 5;
    yPos = yPos - 5;
    $('body').css({ backgroundPosition: xPos +
      'px ' +  yPos + 'px' });
}
```

2. Save this file as `background-auto-diagonal.html`, and view it in your web browser.

Previewing the animation should look like this:

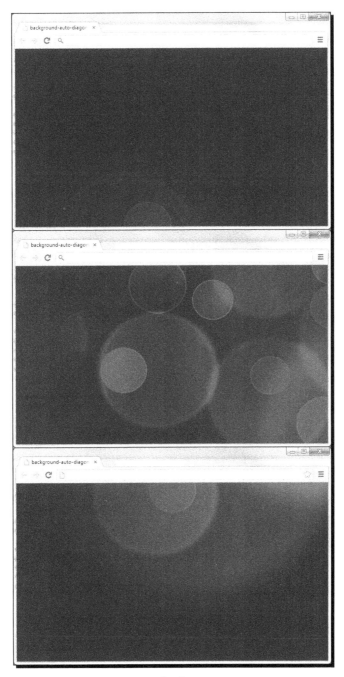

What just happened?

Using the same code, we gave it a bit of an upgrade to allow us to animate both the X coordinates in addition to the Y coordinates of the background position. The variable xPos was added to control the left and right horizontal position and also added to the backgroundPostion line, as well.

Have a go hero

In our example mentioned previously, we made the background image animate northwest. Have a go at making the background animation move northeast, southeast, and southwest. Also, try using the different offset values for the xPos and yPos that aren't the same to see how it affects the background image animation direction.

Parallax background on page elements

Our next example will show you how to animate an element's background position based on the interaction of the window's scroll. This animation can be hard to see based on how smooth scrolling looks in your browser and how smooth the scroll wheel on your mouse is. If you aren't seeing a smooth scroll effect, just grab the scroll bar on your browser and slowly move it up and down to see the effect more clearly. You'll notice that the background position moves at a slower rate than the elements on the page.

Time for action – setting up the markup and styling

To begin, we'll need to add the necessary HTML and CSS to a new document.

1. Create a new HTML page using the same template as before and insert the following code into the `<body>`:

```
<div class="row row1">
  <img src="images/image1.png">
</div>

<div class="row row2">
  <img src="images/image2.png">
</div>

<div class="row row3">
  <img src="images/image3.png">
</div>
```

2. Save the page in the jquery-animation directory as parallax-vertical.html.

3. Next, we should create the stylesheet that we just linked to. In a new file, add the following code:

```
html, body {
    margin:0;
    padding:0;
}
img {
    display:block;
    width:1000px;
    margin:0 auto;
    padding-top:200px;
}
.row { height:700px; }
.row1 { background:url(images/background1.jpg) repeat-x top
  center fixed;}
.row2 { background:url(images/background2.jpg) repeat-x top
  center fixed;}
.row3 { background:url(images/background3.jpg) repeat-x top
  center fixed;}
```

4. Save this file as `parallax-vertical.css` in the `css` folder within our `project` folder.

What just happened?

First, we added in our HTML structure for the example. This consists of three rows holding only one image each. The CSS is pretty straightforward, as well. We're first removing all of the space around the `html` and `body` elements. Then, we set the width and position of the images. We then set the height of the rows, to give us a little space to be able to see the effect. In the wild, this will generally be spaced out by the element's content. Lastly, we set a background image on each of the rows, so that we can see a little variety in our example.

Time for action – scripting our parallax script

Now, let's add in the code that'll make our background animate when we scroll down the page.

1. Add the following code to our anonymous function so we can get this script off the ground and running:

```
$(window).scroll(function() {
    var yPos = -($(window).scrollTop() / 2);
    $(".row").css({ backgroundPosition: "50% " + yPos + "px" });
});
```

Here's a screenshot illustration of how our script will function when previewed in the browser:

What just happened?

We used a window scroll function here because we want to trigger our code every time our user scrolls through the window using the mouse wheel or the browser's scroll bar.

Our variable, yPos, is set to a negative value because we want the background animation to move in the same direction as the page elements that are being scrolled. Using scrollTop() gives us the current vertical scrollbar position of window. We then divide that number by two.

We use the css() method to set our background position. The value 50% is for the x axis, which is the horizontal axis of our browser. This tells our background image to center itself vertically. The y axis (or yPos in this case) is set to our above variable, yPos, and then px is appended to tell the script this number is in pixels. The yPos controls the horizontal placement of the image, and therefore centers the background image horizontally.

Have a go hero – customizing the speed and direction of the effect

Try changing the value of the number yPos is divided by, and then try changing the negative number to a positive number. Changing these values affect the speed and direction that our background position scrolls.

Pop quiz – the scroll() and scrollTop() methods

Q1. What does the scroll() method do?

1. Scrolls to the next sibling element in the set
2. Allows you to smoothly scroll to an element or numerical value (in pixels) on the page
3. Allows code to be run each time the selected element is scrolled
4. When set to false, enables disabled scrolling on the page

Q2. What does the scrollTop() method do?

1. Jumps back to the top of the page
2. Outputs the current scroll position of the selected element
3. When used with the click() method, allows you to scroll to the top of an element
4. Animates the selected element to roll up like a piece of paper

Summary

In this chapter, we looked at several examples that animate the background image on an element. Some of the things we learned were:

- The `animate()` method and some of the great things we can achieve with it
- Using jQuery UI to give our script color animation support
- Fading between background colors on elements
- Chaining jQuery methods together
- Parallax animations, where the background layers are animated at different speeds and directions to create the illusion of depth
- Creating an automatic background image animation and how to make them animate in different directions
- The `scroll()` and `scrollTop()` methods

In the next chapter, we're going to look at navigation animation and how we can bring some life to this common website feature. We're going to be creating a one page scroller script that jumps to sections in the page based on the link clicked. Also, we're going to be looking at how to change the background color of an element to bring attention to that area of the site.

4

Navigation Animation

In this chapter, we're going to look at some animation methods for navigation. Navigation allows our users to move around to different pages in our site. Adding a bit of animation to this common website feature will spice up our web projects. Spicy is good!

Here's a look at the things we'll be learning in this chapter:

- Adding and removing a CSS class to an element when our mouse pointer enters and leaves the element
- Changing the styles of a hovered element using the `animate()` method, along with specifying a duration
- Learning how to smoothly scroll the window to a page element
- We're going to make an example that smoothly scrolls and changes the page background color when a link is clicked. Fancy!

Creating simple navigation animations

We're going to start by simply changing the background color on an anchor tag (`<a>`) when we hover over it. This is the simplest form of navigation animation, so this is a good place to start. We're going to change the background color by adding a class to the element. This will easily allow us to build in more styles to the class if needed.

 We'll be using jQuery UI again in this chapter to make up for the lack of support for color animation in jQuery 2.0. Refer to the previous chapter on where to download the jQuery UI library.

Configuring addClass() and removeClass()

The syntax of addClass() and removeClass() may look like the following (square brackets denote optional arguments):

```
$(selector).addClass( className [,duration] [,easing] [,complete] );
$(selector).removeClass( className [,duration] [,easing] [,complete]
  );
```

 It's important to note that duration isn't a jQuery option on addClass() or removeClass(). This option is being added in by the jQuery UI and is called a method override.

Time for action – setting up our navigation

Let's create our navigation structure and basic animation by performing the following steps:

1.   We'll start by creating a new document based on our template file from the first chapter, naming it navigation-animation1.html and saving it in our jquery-animation directory.

2.   Next, we'll need to add the jQuery UI library after our jQuery library by adding this line:

     ```
     <script src="js/jquery-ui.min.js"></script>
     ```

3.   Then, we will add the following HTML code into our newly created document under the <body> tag:

     ```
     <nav>
       <a href="#">Link1</a>
       <a href="#">Link2</a>
       <a href="#">Link3</a>
       <a href="#">Link4</a>
       <a href="#">Link5</a>
       <a href="#">Link6</a>
       <a href="#">Link7</a>
     </nav>
     ```

4. Save the following code to a file `navigation-animation1.css` and link it to our HTML document:

```
nav a {
  display:block;
  float:left;
  padding:5px 10px;
  background:#DDD;
}
nav a.hover {background:#F0F;}
```

5. Add this code into our empty anonymous function so we can get our script moving:

```
$("nav a").hover(function(){
  $(this).addClass("hover", 300);
}, function(){
  $(this).removeClass("hover", 300);
});
```

What just happened?

We used the `hover()` handler to tell our navigation link what to do when our mouse cursor enters and leaves the element. We also set the duration to `300` (milliseconds) so the `hover()` method animation is slightly delayed and gives us the animation effect we want.

The following screenshot is an illustration of how the animation should work by moving the cursor from the first link through the last one:

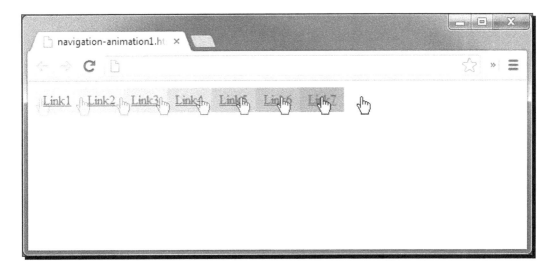

Have a go hero – extending our hover style

Have a go and see what other effects can be achieved by adding additional styles to our `hover` class. For starters, try changing the element's `height` and `position`.

Using the stop() method

The previous example is a simple way to allow for easy updates to the styles. You'll notice that if you hover over all the navigation links very quickly, going back and forth several times and then stop, the animation continues until it's played out each animation. This isn't generally a very desirable effect, so we need to add the `stop()` method to stop the previous animation before the next one starts. We need to adjust our code a bit since `addClass()` and `removeClass()` can't be stopped in the animation queue. For this, we'll be using the `animate()` method to allow us to stop the animations.

Time for action – adding the stop() method

To stop our animations before the next one starts, we'll need to modify our code a little. Adding `stop()` before the `animate()` effect is what we'll need to do.

Using the same file as before (`navigation-animation1.html`), we're going to update the code in our anonymous function with the following code (the new code is highlighted):

```
$("nav a").hover(function(){
  $(this).stop().animate({ backgroundColor:"#F0F" }, 300);
}, function(){
  $(this).stop().animate({ backgroundColor:"#DDD" }, 300);
});
```

What just happened?

You'll notice that if we quickly move our pointer over the navigation links now (moving our cursor back and forth), the previous animation stops before the next one starts. This is a much more elegant animation than the previous one. Just like spicy, we like elegant too.

Animating the window with scrollTop()

In the previous chapter, we learned how to use `scrollTop()` to make the background image of our `<body>` element animate on the page in different directions and speeds. In the next example, we're going to use `scrollTop()` to animate the window by smoothly scrolling to an element on the page.

The *smooth scrolling* animation method can be used to visually indicate to our users that the position of our window has changed based on an action they take on the page, generally following a mouse click of an element. This animation method is often used exactly as we're going to build it and is referred to as a *one pager*.

Time for action – scripting our smooth scrolling animation

In the following steps, we're going to create our smooth-scrolling, one pager animation that will animate to different sections of the content in our page:

1. First, let's start by making a new file using our template smooth-scrolling.html, and then saving it in our jquery-animation folder.

2. Second, we're going to add in our jQuery UI library again by inserting the following code directly below our jQuery library (the new code has been highlighted):

```
<script src="js/jquery.js"></script>
<script src="js/jquery-ui.min.js"></script>
```

3. Next, we need to add the following CSS code to a new file named smooth-scrolling.css and link it in smooth-scrolling.html:

```
body, html {
  margin:0;
  padding:0;
}
body {background:#CCC;}
nav {
  width:100%;
  position:fixed;
  top:0;
  padding:10px 0;
  text-align:center;
  outline:1px dotted #FFF;
  background:#EEE;
  background-color:rgba(255, 255, 255, 0.9);
}
nav a {
  color:#222;
  margin:0 10px;
  text-decoration:none;
}
content {margin-top:50px;}
content div {
  height:400px;
```

```
      margin:10px;
      padding:10px;
      outline:1px solid #FFF;
      background:#EEE;
      background-color:rgba(255, 255, 255, 0.8);
   }
```

4. Then, we'll add the following HTML code under the `<body>` tag:

```
<nav>
   <a href="#link1">Link1</a>
   <a href="#link2">Link2</a>
   <a href="#link3">Link3</a>
   <a href="#link4">Link4</a>
   <a href="#link5">Link5</a>
   <a href="#link6">Link6</a>
   <a href="#link7">Link7</a>
</nav>

<div class="content">
   <div id="link1">Link1</div>
   <div id="link2">Link2</div>
   <div id="link3">Link3</div>
   <div id="link4">Link4</div>
   <div id="link5">Link5</div>
   <div id="link6">Link6</div>
   <div id="link7">Link7</div>
</div>
```

5. Finally, add the following to our anonymous function:

```
$("a[href^='#']").click(function(e){
   var pos = $(this.hash).offset().top - 50;
   $("body, html").stop().animate({ scrollTop:pos }, 1000);
   e.preventDefault();
});
```

What just happened?

We used the `click()` handler with a complicated looking selector. The selector we used means: select all anchor tags (`<a>`) whose `href` attribute begins with (^) a pound sign (#).

Our selector will be the `<body>` tag for this example and we're using the `animate()` method to handle our dirty work. The `stop()` method is used again so the previous animation stops before the next one begins. We're setting a new variable named `pos` to hold the position of the clicked link (`<a>`) from the top of the page using `offset().top`. Also, we're subtracting `50` from the `pos` variable as an offset because we want the top of the `content` element to land just under the navigation bar. We set the duration of the animation to `1000` milliseconds, because we want it to take 1 second for the animation to jump from the current position on the page to the next.

Smooth scrolling and page background color

Now, let's take the two animation methods we learned above and merge them together into one. This example will use the smooth scrolling method to jump to our linked elements and change the page background color at the same time.

The following screenshot illustrates the stopping points of the corresponding links after they're clicked in our navigation bar:

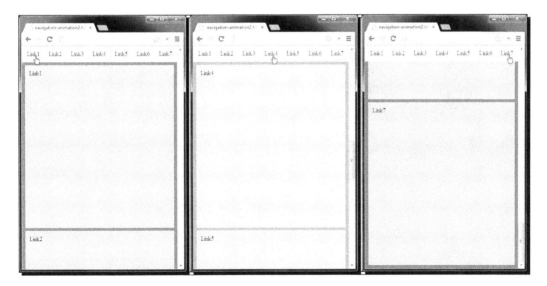

Time for action – creating the super animation

To merge our previous two examples together, we'll need to create a new file and mix our CSS and jQuery code from both the examples together. Of course, we'll need to make a few adjustments to allow them to work together.

1. Create a new document called `navigation-animation2.html` using the file template and save it under our `jquery-animation` folder.

2. Then, place the following CSS code into a new file called `navigation-animation2.css`, and link it in the HTML document we just created:

```css
body, html {
  margin:0;
  padding:0;
}
body {background:#F00;}
nav {
  width:100%;
  position:fixed;
  top:0;
  padding:10px 0;
  text-align:center;
  outline:1px solid #FFF;
  background:#EEE;
  background-color:rgba(255, 255, 255, 0.5);
}
nav a {
  color:#222;
  margin:0 10px;
  text-decoration:none;
}
content {margin-top:50px;}
content div {
  height:400px;
  margin:10px;
  padding:10px;
  outline:1px solid #FFF;
  background:#EEE;
  background-color:rgba(255, 255, 255, 0.8);
}
```

3. Finally, we need to place the following code into our anonymous function:

```
$("a[href^='#']").click(function(e){
  e.preventDefault();
  var link = $(this).index() + 1;
  var background = "";

  if (link == 1) {
    background = "#F00"          //red
  } else if (link == 2) {
    background = "#FF5000"       //orange
  } else if (link == 3) {
    background = "#FF0"          //yellow
  } else if (link == 4) {
    background = "#0F0"          //green
  } else if (link == 5) {
    background = "#0FF"          //light blue
  } else if (link == 6) {
    background = "#00F"          //dark blue
  } else if (link == 7) {
    background = "#F0F"          //fuschia
  }

  var pos = $(this.hash).offset().top - 50;
  $("body, html").stop().animate({ scrollTop:pos,
    backgroundColor:background }, 1000);
});
```

What just happened?

The first thing we did was add a new `link` variable. This will hold the index value of the link that our user clicks on. We incremented the index value by 1 because the `index()` method is zero-based, and it's been a long day, so we don't want to deal with starting at zero when we count up.

The `background` variable is declared to ward off those filthy JavaScript error monsters, as always. We created an `if` statement to handle the hex values of background colors. The `background` variable gets set to the color (that we defined) of the link that's clicked.

Our selector for this magic trick will be the `<body>` tag again, because we're both scrolling to another position on the page and changing the background color of the page as well. This is the same code as before, except this time, we added `backgroundColor` and are setting the value (background) from the if statement above.

Have a go hero – extending the script further

Try to think of some added functionality to our merged animation example. Here are a few ideas to get you going:

◆ Dynamically change the height of the content `<div>` elements to the height of the window (don't forget to add in a window resize function)

◆ Change the background color using a window scroll function so that it changes colors if you manually scroll down the page and not just by clicking on the links

◆ Fade in the content `<div>` elements once they come into view either by clicking on the links or by manually scrolling down the page

◆ Automatically scroll through the content without having to click on the links

Pop quiz – the ^ symbol and the stop() method

Q1. What does the ^ symbol mean in our `<a>` selector?

1. It means "equals"

2. It means "contains"

3. It means "starts with"

4. It means "ends with"

Q2. What does the `stop()` method do?

1. It stops the animation queue on the selected element(s)

2. It stops the page from loading

3. It stops all the animations on the page

4. It stops animations from running until the page is reloaded

Summary

In this chapter, we learned how to change the styles on an element based on our mouse interactions, using `addClass()` and `removeClass()`, and how to control the speed (duration) of adding and removing those classes with a little help from jQuery UI's method overrides.

Then, we learned how to smoothly scroll the window to a specified element on our page. Later, we merged both of our examples together into one example that would smoothly scroll the window and fade our page's background color. Also in this chapter, we found a puppy. What's that? You didn't find a puppy? You must have missed a semi-colon somewhere.

Now that we've added a little spice to our navigation elements, we're going to learn how to give some life to our form inputs in the next chapter. Some of the things we'll learn in the next chapter are form validation animation, visually changing the form to alert the user of a problem with their submission, and how to shake the form if we need the user to fix one of their entries.

5
Form and Input Animation

In this chapter, we will look at examples and concepts of form animation using jQuery. We can use almost any animation type for animating form inputs (because of quirks and compatibility). However, keep in mind that a lot of animations won't make sense or will confuse our user, so we'll be steering clear of those. These animation types are ones that are too "jarring" to the eye. For example, if we change the dimensions of the form inputs, our user might not know what it means. For our first examples, we're going to be sticking with color changes mostly. Later in the chapter, we'll strap on more animation support using jQuery UI to really get our forms moving!

In our examples for this chapter, we'll be creating HTML forms so that we can get the visual representation of form animation. For these examples, we won't be adding a form action because we don't need them to submit properly.

In this chapter we will cover the following topics:

◆ Animating the form when our user moves their mouse cursor over the form fields

◆ Changing the background color of the input fields once our user clicks on one of them

◆ Animating the form's appearance based on the form validation

These are the event handlers we'll be using in this chapter to get our form elements moving:

◆ `hover()`

◆ `focus()`

◆ `blur()`

Using simple form animations

Form animations can be used for many reasons, most notably when our user interacts with our form. More specifically, forms can be used when his or her cursor enters or leaves our form elements (text box). Animations are also great for indicating form validation errors. These animations will generally have slight color changes on the form inputs to give our user a better experience when filling out the form and to make the flow easier to follow.

 We'll be using jQuery UI again in this chapter to make up for the lack of support for color animation in jQuery 2.0. Refer to *Chapter 3*, *Background Animation*, on where to download the jQuery UI library.

Time for action – creating the form

We will be creating an HTML form using the following steps. After we create our form, we'll be adding in our form validation animation.

1. Start by creating a new document using our template (from *Chapter 1*, *Getting Started*) called `form-animation.html` and save it in our `jquery-animation` folder.

2. Then we'll place the following code inside our `<body>` tag:

```
<form id="form1">
  <input type="text" placeholder="First Name">
  <input type="text" placeholder="Last Name">
  <input type="text" placeholder="Email Address">
  <input type="text" placeholder="Phone Number">
  <input type="submit" value="Submit">
</form>
```

3. We'll then need to add the jQuery UI library, following our jQuery library, by adding the following code. (See information box mentioned previously on where to get the jQuery UI library):

```
<script src="js/jquery-ui.min.js"></script>
```

4. In our anonymous function, add in the following code:

```
$("input").hover(
  function() {
    $(this).addClass("hover", 500);
  },
  function() {
    $(this).removeClass("hover", 500);
```

```
  }
);

$("input").focus(function() {
  $(this).addClass("focus", 500);
});

$("input").blur(function() {
  $(this).removeClass("focus", 500);
});
```

5. Create a new file called `form-animation.css`, save it under our `jquery-animation` folder, and add the following code:

```
form {
  float:left;
  margin:5px;
}
input {
  display:block;
  width:200px;
  padding:10px;
  border-radius:3px;
  background:#F5F5F5;
  border:1px solid #D5D5D5;
}
input[type=submit] {
  width:auto;
  border:0;
  color:#FFF;
  text-transform:uppercase;
}
input:focus {outline:0;}
#form1 input[type=submit] {
  background:#FF6B6B;
  border:1px solid #FF3A3A;
}
```

Attribute selectors (`input[type=submit]`) are a little quirky in Legacy versions of Internet Explorer. Make sure your selectors are supported (or polyfill them) before using them.

Here's a great list of HTML5 cross-browser polyfills: `https://github.com/Modernizr/Modernizr/wiki/HTML5-Cross-browser-Polyfills`.

At this point, our form should look like the following screenshot:

What just happened?

The first section of code we added in is the HTML skeleton structure we'll use for the code examples in this chapter. We used an ID on the form for general targeting purposes. We'll change this ID later in the chapter once we add another form. Obviously, these forms don't have an action as we don't need them to submit in order to see our animations.

Secondly, we added in the jQuery UI library to support color animation and give us duration options for `addClass()` and `removeClass()`, and to add color animation as we did in the previous chapters.

The jQuery code we added next are the handlers we need for animating the styles on our form by adding and removing CSS classes to our input elements. The `hover()` handler has a `mouseenter` and `mouseleave` event. This is helpful in keeping our code together in the same function. The jQuery equivalent to `onFocus` and `onBlur` in JavaScript is `focus()` and `blur()`. Unlike `hover()`, these handlers have to be separated.

Time for action – adding our animation styles to the form

We've added all of the code we needed for our forms; now, let's add some styles to our form to get the animation styles working.

1. Add this code near the bottom of the stylesheet we created named
    `form-animation.css` between the styles for `input:focus` and
    `#form1 input[type=submit]`:

    ```
    #form1 input.hover {border:1px solid #FF7F7F;}
      #form1 input.focus {
      background:#FFD8D8;
      border:1px solid #FF7F7F;
    }
    ```

What just happened?

Now, let's preview the form with our newly added styles and take it for a spin. You'll notice that when you hover over each of the text inputs, that a red border slowly fades in and slowly fades out when we move our mouse cursor off of the text input. Clicking on the text inputs will now fade the background color to red as well. When we click away from the focused input, the red background color then slowly fades back to its original color.

 These animations can also be achieved using CSS3 transitions.

The order of the CSS styles we added is very important. The first state is the `hover` state, so these styles go first. We want the focus class to override the `hover` state while it's in transition between animations, so it goes under the hover styles.

Lastly, the submit button's styles go on the last line because we don't want the styles to change when you hover over it. If you aren't familiar with this method of ordering styles and why it's important, read up on CSS specificity. Swapping the order of the styles we just added will illustrate why the order is important.

Form validation animations

Validating our user's form submission is a great way to ensure we get back the correct information from our users. To enhance the usability of our form, we're going to cover a few animation methods that deal with form validation. We're going to start with basic form validation and build from there.

Time for action – basic dialog form validation

We're going to create form validation through the use of an alert to tell the user what's wrong with the form's submission.

1. First off, we'll need to place the following code inside our anonymous function after our previously added code:

```
$("#form1 input[type=submit]").click(function(e) {
  e.preventDefault();
  var msg_error = "";
  $("#form1 input[type=text]").each(function() {
    if ($(this).val() == "") {
      msg_error += $(this).attr("placeholder") +
        "can't be left blank.\n";
    }
```

```
  });

  if (msg_error) {
    alert(msg_error);
  } else {
    alert("Form submitted successfully!");
  }
});
```

What just happened?

We used the `click()` handler on our submit button to trigger our form validation checking. For the sake of this example, we used `preventDefault()` so that when we click on our submit button, the URL hash doesn't change. Make sure to remove this line when you launch this code into the wilds of the Internet.

The `each()` method is used to target all of the form inputs in our form. An if statement is used to narrow it down to all inputs (by using `$(this)` since we're already in the `each()` method), whose value is blank. Each time our `if` statement returns true, we're going to add to the variable `msg_error`. We used the blank input's placeholder value we set previously as the first part of our error message. We added on `can't be left blank` for the rest of the validation error message and end it with a new line (`\n`), so that all of the error messages aren't on the same line in the dialog window.

Lastly, we need to make sure if there is even an error message to display, so we check if our `msg_error` variable returns `true`. If it is, we'll use `alert()` with our variable `msg_error` inside to throw the dialog window. Otherwise, we'll use `alert()` to let the user know the form was successfully submitted.

Have a go hero – extending our form validation

For this example, we used very basic form validation to make sure that none of our input fields were left blank. Have a go at extending the script to check different types of values. Some examples of these validation types are:

- Contains only numbers
- Contains only letters
- Contains a certain amount of characters
- Contains only letters and is within a certain range (example: 1-100)
- Date is in the future

Time for action – animating form validation errors

Now, instead of giving our users a dialog box of all of the validation errors, we're going to visually point out the form field errors that need to be fixed.

1. We'll start by adding a new form to our page. Add the following code right after our first `<form>` (new code is highlighted):

    ```
    <form id="form2">
        <input type="text" placeholder="First Name">
        <input type="text" placeholder="Last Name">
        <input type="text" placeholder="Email Address">
        <input type="text" placeholder="Phone Number">
        <input type="submit" value="Submit">
    </form>
    ```

2. Next, we'll add in our new form styles by placing the following code at the bottom of our stylesheet:

    ```
    #form2 input.hover {border:1px solid #7FA1D1;}
    #form2 input.focus {
      background:#E6F0FF;
      border:1px solid #7FA1D1;
    }
    #form2 input[type=submit] {
      background:#8FACD7;
      border:1px solid #638CC7;
    }
    #form2 input.error {border:1px dashed #F00;}
    ```

3. Let's then add in the code that'll be used to check our form for proper validation:

    ```
    $("#form2 input[type=submit]").click(function(e) {
        e.preventDefault();
        $("#form2 input[type=text]").each(function() {
            if ($(this).val() == "") {
                $(this).addClass("error");
            } else {
                $(this).removeClass("error");
            }
        });
    });
    ```

What just happened?

We used the same code as the previous example, but instead of triggering a dialog box with all of the input validation errors, we changed the border color to a dashed red border for each of the text inputs that require some attention before they can be passed through the form. Our old friends `addClass()` and `removeClass()` were used to style the inputs that had errors by adding or removing the class `"error"`.

Have a go hero – putting it all together

Now have a go at putting together all of the form validation animation types we just learned. Also, try extending the styles a bit more. Here are some ideas for extending the styles and animations:

♦ Display an error message on the side of the form field as to what the validation error is.

♦ Display a background image inside the form field to signify a problem with the submission.

♦ Automatically set the cursor focus to the first form field that has a validation error.

♦ If your form has labels (as opposed to placeholders), change the color of the respective label.

♦ Make the form fields that have validation errors pulsate to continuously signify an error (using border colors and/or background colors).

Try playing with some jQuery UI animation effects on your own and come up with some swanky animations. We'll learn more about all of the great things jQuery UI can do in *Chapter 6, Extending Animations with jQuery UI*, but here's one jQuery UI animation to get your feet wet:

```
$("form").effect("bounce", { direction:"left", easing:"linear" },
  500);
```

Pop quiz – form animation and jQuery UI

Q1. When is it acceptable to use form animation?

1. When we want to direct our user's attention to a specific area of the form

2. When our user interacts with our form

3. To enhance the user's experience of our form

4. All of the above

Q2. Why did we add in jQuery UI in our examples in this chapter?

1. To give us the ability to use animation effects not native to jQuery

2. To add the `duration` option to `addClass()` and `removeClass()` and give us the ability to animate color

3. To allow us to use smooth scrolling options for `scrollTop()`

4. To make `preventDefault()` work properly for our examples

Summary

In this chapter we learned how to visually change the form's appearance based on the interaction with the form. To take this a step further, you can create custom animations using other CSS styles, altering the element using jQuery or by using jQuery UI effects. Just remember — don't make the animations too sudden or abrupt. Form animations are generally used to help a user through the flow of filling out the form. Make sure to walk through each form step and animation as if you are a user who is filling out the form for the very first time.

In the next chapter, we're going to be looking at the great animation effects that can be added by using jQuery UI on top of the jQuery library. jQuery UI is great because not only does it add new animation effects, but it adds in additional options for native jQuery methods.

6

Extended Animations with jQuery UI

jQuery UI is the official user interface library for jQuery and adds a suite of interactive widgets such as tabs and accordions, a series of interaction helpers such as drag and drop, and a comprehensive set of effects that extend those provided natively by jQuery.

Over the course of this chapter, we'll be looking at the additional effects added by jQuery UI. Topics we'll cover include:

- Obtaining and setting up jQuery UI
- The new effects added by jQuery UI
- Using the `effect()` method
- Extending the `show()`, `hide()`, and `toggle()` methods
- Using easing with jQuery UI
- Animating an element's color
- Animated class transitions

jQuery UI adds several new animation methods, as well as modifying several jQuery methods. The methods that we'll be looking at in this chapter are:

- `animate()`
- `addClass()`
- `effect()`
- `hide()`
- `switchClass()`
- `show()`
- `toggle()`

Obtaining and setting up jQuery UI

jQuery UI is very easy to obtain and set up. There is an online tool that will build a custom download package for us containing just the parts of jQuery UI that we'll need. Due to the modular nature of jQuery UI it makes sense to minimize the code payload we use on any given web project, and so the ability to include only the modules of code we intend to use helps us to minimize any impact on the visitor our code may have.

The jQuery UI download builder can be found at `http://jqueryui.com/download`. The page is split into two sections with the components of the library listed towards the top and the theme details at the bottom. The download builder has a certain amount of intelligence, and will ensure that any dependencies are automatically selected when we choose the components we require.

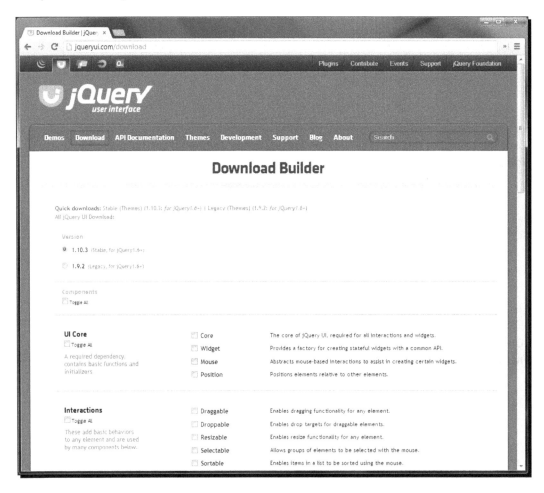

The **Download Builder** page shown in the previous screenshot gives us everything we need to run any subset of the library components.

All we'll be using in this chapter are the effects, so when we download a package we should only select the components found in the **Effects** subsection towards the bottom of the page. We don't need to include a theme, and we don't even need to include the library core. The effects can be used completely independent of the rest of the library; all we need is the **Effects Core** file and the individual effects we require. Make sure all of them are selected, and download the package.

The download builder allows you to only download the pieces you need, because jQuery UI is basically an add-on. Breaking apart each piece, allows you to select only the pieces you need, which greatly cuts down on the file size of the plugin when customized.

The package will give us everything we need to use the components that we've selected, including a copy of the latest stable release of jQuery, so when using jQuery UI, jQuery itself does not need to be downloaded separately.

All of the JavaScript for each selected component is combined and compressed into a single file by the download builder, and any functional CSS or theme files will be combined into a single stylesheet. We don't need any of the theme files for working with the effects, but ensure the `.js` file from the archive provided by the download builder goes into our `js` folder.

Creating a new template file

The examples in the remainder of this chapter will be short, mostly image-based examples that illustrate each effect in turn, so it makes sense to use a slightly different template file for them. Create a new template file by adding a reference to the jQuery UI source file directly after the jQuery one just before the closing `</body>` tag.

The new effects added by jQuery UI

At the time of writing, jQuery UI gives us 14 new, predefined animation effects to use in our pages; these are listed, together with a brief description of their usage, as follows:

Animations	Description
blind	The target element is shown or hidden by rolling it down or up like a window blind.
bounce	The target element is bounced horizontally or vertically for a specified number of times.
clip	The target element is shown or hidden by moving opposing edges in towards the center of the element, or out to its full width or height.
drop	The element appears to drop onto or off of the page in order to show or hide it respectively.
explode	The explode effect causes the target element to separate into a specified number of pieces before fading away, or to fade into view in several pieces before coming together to form the complete element.
fold	The element appears to fold closed or open.
highlight	The background-color property of the target element is set (to yellow by default, although this is configurable), and then fades away after a short interval.
puff	The target element increases in size slightly and then fades away.
pulsate	The target element's opacity is adjusted a specified number of times, making the element appear to flicker on and off.
scale	The dimensions of the target element are adjusted to increase or decrease its size.
shake	The target element is shaken a specified number of times. This effect is similar to the bounce effect with the key difference being that the distance of the shake remains the same on each iteration of the animation.
size	The dimensions of the target element are adjusted to increase or decrease its size. This effect is almost identical to scale.
slide	The target element is made to slide in or out of view, horizontally or vertically.
transfer	The outline of the specified element is transferred to another element on the page.

Using the effect API

jQuery UI introduces the effect() method, which can be used to trigger any of the effects listed in the previous table. The effect() method's usage pattern is as follows:

```
$(selector).effect( effect [,options] [,duration] [,complete] );
```

The name of the effect that we would like to use is always the first argument of the `effect()` method. It's supplied in the string format.

Each effect has custom configuration options that can be set to control how the effect displays. These options are set in a configuration object which is passed to the `effect()` method as the second argument, following the name of the effect.

We can also supply a duration for the effect as an argument. Just like standard jQuery animations, we can supply either an integer representing the duration of the effect in milliseconds, or one of the strings `slow` or `fast`.

If no configuration is required, the duration may be passed to the `effect()` method as the second argument. If no duration is supplied, the default duration of `400` milliseconds will be used.

Optionally, a callback function may be provided as the final argument. The supplied function will be executed once for each selected element when the effect ends.

Let's look at a few examples of how the `effect()` method can be used.

The bounce effect

The `bounce` effect is similar to, but much more controllable than, the `easeOutBounce` easing function. It can be used with either the effect API or show/hide logic depending on your requirements.

Syntax

```
$(selector).effect( "bounce" [,configuration] [,duration] );
```

Configuration options

The following configuration options are available for the bounce effect:

Option	Default	Usage
direction	"up"	The direction of bounce. The other possible option is the string down
distance	20	The initial distance of bounce (successive bounces reduce in distance) in pixels
mode	"effect"	Whether to run the effect normally or use the show/hide logic, other values accepted may be the strings show, hide, or toggle
times	5	The number of bounces

Time for action – using the bounce effect

In this example we'll see how the jQuery UI effect can be combined to create a bouncing ball that travels across the page:

1. Use the following simple elements in the `<body>` of the template file:

```
<div id="travel">
  <div id="ball"></div>
</div>
```

2. All we need is a simple container `<div>` and an inner `<div>`. In the empty function at the end of the `<body>`, add the following script:

```
$("#ball").click(function() {
$("#travel").animate({
  left: "+=300px"
  }, 1500).find("div").effect( "bounce", { times: 4,
  distance: 100 }, 1500 );
});
```

3. Save the file as `bounce.html`. We also need a few simple styles. Add the following CSS to a new file:

```
#travel {
  position:absolute;
  top:100px;
}
#ball {
  width:150px;
  height:150px;
  cursor:pointer;
  background:url(../img/ball.jpg) no-repeat 0 0;
}
```

4. Save this as `bounce.css` in the `css` folder. When we run the page and click on the ball, we should find that it bounces along the page, gradually coming to a halt:

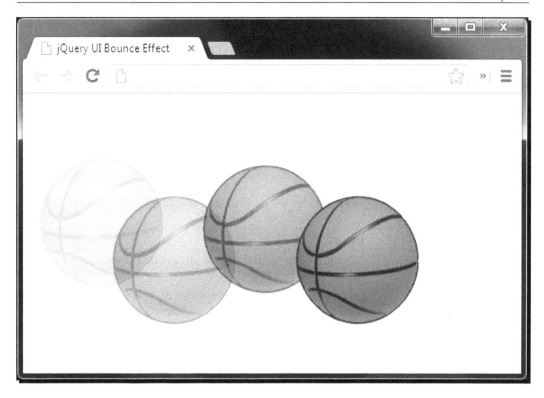

The previous composition shows the ball traveling across the page, bouncing up and down as it goes from left to right.

What just happened?

When the ball is clicked, we first use jQuery's `animate()` method to animate the `left` style property of the container, `#travel`, by 300 pixels, over a duration of 1.5 seconds. We slow this animation down to improve the appearance of the overall animation, but it is not strictly required. We then navigate down to the inner `<div>` element and use the `effect()` method, specifying the `bounce` effect.

We need to use both elements, `#travel` and `#ball`, because if we use the `animate()` and `effect()` methods on the same element, the bounce effect will go into the element's animation queue and the two animations will execute one after the other instead of running simultaneously.

The highlight effect

The `highlight` effect is a simple but effective way to draw the visitor's attention to new items that have been added to the page, and is used for this purpose in many of today's leading web-based interfaces.

Syntax

```
$(selector).effect( "highlight" [,configuration] [,duration] );
```

Configuration options

There are only two configuration options for the `highlight` effect; these are listed as follows:

Options	Default	Usage
color	"#ffff99"	Sets the background-color property of the element being highlighted
mode	"show"	Sets whether the effect will be hidden or shown when used with the effect() method, other possible values include hide, toggle, or effect

Time for action – highlighting elements

In this example we'll create a simple to-do list, with a series of default items that can be checked off. We can also allow new items to be added to the list and will apply the `highlight` effect to new items as they are added.

1. Add the following HTML code to the <body> element of the template file:

```
<div id="todo">
  <h2>Todo List</h2>
  <ul>
    <li><label><input type="checkbox">Item 1</label></li>
    <li><label><input type="checkbox">Item 2</label></li>
    <li><label><input type="checkbox">Item 3</label></li>
  </ul>
  <input type="text" id="new">
  <button id="add">Add</button>
</div>
```

2. Add the behavior for our to-do list using the following code:

```
$("#add").click(function() {
  var newItem = $("#new"),
    text = newItem.val();

  if (text) {
    var li = $("<li>"),
      label = $("<label>").html("<input type=\"checkbox\">" +
        text).appendTo(li);
    li.appendTo("#todo ul").effect("highlight", 2000);
    newItem.val("");
  }
  // prevent the form from submitting
  return false;
});
```

3. Save this page as `highlight.html`. We also need some CSS for this example. In a new file in your text editor, add the following code:

```
#todo {
    width:208px;
    font:normal 13px sans-serif;
}
#todo ul {
    padding:0;
    margin-bottom:30px;
}
#todo li { list-style-type:none; }
#todo label {
    display:block;
    border-bottom:1px dotted #000;
}
li input {
    position:relative;
    top:2px;
}
input { margin-right:10px; }
```

4. Save this page as `highlight.css`.

5. When we run the page in a browser, we can add a new item and it will be highlighted briefly as the new item is added to the list:

In the previous screenshot we see the fade effect before it fades away from the newly added item.

What just happened?

We add a click handler to the `<button>` element at the bottom of the list, which drives the functionality of the rest of the behavior. When the `<button>` element is clicked, we cache the selector for the `<input>` field and obtain the text that was entered into it.

If the variable holding the text is not empty, we then create new `<label>` and `<input>` elements. We add the text to the `<label>` element, as well, and then append the new item to the list. Finally, we apply the `highlight` effect and empty the `<input>` field.

The pulsate effect

The `pulsate` effect fades the element in and out of view a specified number of times so that the target element appears to pulsate. Like most of the effects we have looked at so far, it is easy to use and requires little or no configuration.

Syntax

```
$(selector).effect( "pulsate", [,configuration] [,duration] );
```

Configuration options

The `pulsate` effect also has just two configurable options; these are shown in the following table:

Option	Default	Usage
mode	"show"	Sets whether the target element is shown or hidden when used with the `effect()` method, other possible values include `hide`, `toggle`, and `effect`
times	5	Sets the number of times the target element is pulsated

Time for action – making an element pulsate

In this example, we'll show a simple time sheet in which rows can be deleted by clicking a link. If a link is clicked, the corresponding row will be pulsated before it is removed.

1. Use the following markup in the template file:

```
<table>
  <tr>
    <th>Job Number</th>
    <th>Start Time</th>
    <th>End Time</th>
    <th colspan="2">Total</th>
  </tr>
  <tr>
    <td>05432</td>
    <td>8:00</td>
    <td>8:43</td>
    <td>43 minutes</td>
    <td>
      <a class="delete" href="#" title="Delete this item">
        Delete
      </a>
    </td>
  </tr>
  <tr>
    <td>05684</td>
    <td>8:43</td>
    <td>10:21</td>
    <td>1 hour 38 minutes</td>
    <td>
      <a class="delete" href="#" title="Delete this item">
        Delete
```

```
      </a>
    </td>
  </tr>
  <tr>
    <td>05684</td>
    <td>10:21</td>
    <td>13:30</td>
    <td>3 hour 9 minutes</td>
    <td>
      <a class="delete" href="#" title="Delete this item">
        Delete
      </a>
    </td>
  </tr>
</table>
```

2. Add the code to apply the effect to the closure at the bottom of the page:

```
$(".delete").click(function(e) {
  e.preventDefault();

  var row = $(this).closest("tr");

  row.closest("tr").children().css("backgroundColor",
    "red").effect("pulsate", function() {
  row.remove();
  });
});
```

3. Save this file as `pulsate.html`. Only a couple of styles are required for this example. These should go into a new file:

```
table {
    border-spacing:0;
    font:normal 13px sans-serif;
}
th, td {
    text-align:left;
    padding-right:20px;
}
```

4. Save this file in the `css` folder as `pulsate.css`.

5. Clicking the delete link in any row will apply the `pulsate` effect and then remove the table row:

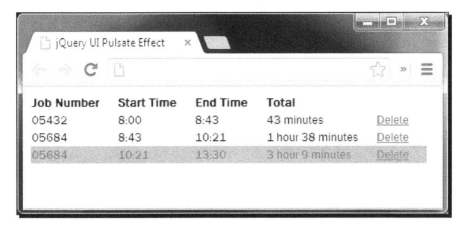

The previous screenshot shows a single `pulsate` animation as it fades out.

What just happened?

When a **Delete** link is clicked on, our handler function first sets the `background-color` property of the `<tr>` element that the link is within. This is not mandatory for the effect, but it does help bring it to life.

We then apply the `pulsate` effect to all of the `<td>` elements within the row using the `effect()` method. We need to apply the effect to the `<td>` elements instead of the `<tr>` element so that the effect works as intended in IE.

When the effect ends, our inline callback function will be executed, which removes the `<tr>` element. Obviously the `<tr>` element can only be removed once, and once it has been removed, subsequent attempts to remove it will just fail silently.

The shake effect

The `shake` effect shakes the element that it is applied back and forth a specified number of times.

Syntax

```
$(selector).effect( "shake", [,configuration] [,duration] );
```

Configuration options

The `shake` effect exposes three configuration options that allow us to customize its behavior.

The configuration options are listed in the following table:

Option	Default	Usage
direction	"left"	Sets the direction that the element moves in
distance	20	Sets the number of pixels the element travels when it is shaken
times	3	Sets the number of times the element shakes

Time for action – shaking an element

The open source CMS WordPress uses the `shake` effect when incorrect login details are entered in the sign-in form for its backend administration area. In this example we can see how easy it is to implement this behavior using the `shake` effect.

1. Add the following markup to the template file as the basis of the login form:

```
<form>
  <h2>Login</h2>
  <label>Username:<input id="name" type="text"></label>
  <label>Password:<input id="pass" type="text"></label>
  <input type="submit" id="submit" value="Login">
</form>
```

2. Now add the following code to the empty closure at the bottom of the template file:

```
$("#submit").click(function(e) {
  e.preventDefault();

  $("input").each(function(i, val) {
    if (!$(this).val()) {
      $(this).css("border", "1px solid red").effect("shake", {
        distance: 5 }, 100);
    }
  });
});
```

3. Save this file as `shake.html`. We also need a basic stylesheet for this example. Add the following CSS to a new file:

```
form {
  width:145px;
  padding:20px;
  margin:auto;
  border:1px solid #000;
  font:normal 13px sans-serif;
}
```

```
h2 {
  font-size:14px;
  margin-top:0;
}
input {
  display:block;
  margin-bottom:10px;
  border:1px solid #000;
}
```

4. Save this file as `shake.css`.

5. If we run the page in a browser and click the **Login** input button without completing either of the `<input>` fields, both fields will have their borders set to red and will shake from side to side:

In the previous screenshot, we see the text fields being shaken when they are left empty and the **Login** button is clicked.

What just happened?

When the **Login** button is clicked we simply check to see if each `<input>` has a value, and if not, we apply a red border and then call the `effect()` method specifying `shake` as the effect. We use a configuration object to reduce the distance the element moves, as well as specifying a relatively short duration.

The size effect

The `size` effect is used to resize an element, making it grow or shrink depending on its configuration. Unlike most of the other effects, the `size` effect must be configured for it to be used successfully.

The `size` effect is also one of the only effects that has the base core file as well as another effect as a dependency. Most components rely only on the core file. As we downloaded the entire effect suite from the jQuery UI download builder, we don't need to worry about including the additional effect. It's already in the single file that the download builder created when we downloaded it at the start of the chapter.

Syntax

```
$(selector).effect( "size", [,configuration] [,duration] );
```

Configuration options

The `size` effect gives us four configurable options, which are listed as follows:

Option	Default	Usage
from	none	Sets the size of the target element at the beginning of the animation. This option accepts an object with the `height` and `width` keys which are used to set the starting size of the target element. This option is not mandatory
to	none	Sets the size of the target element at the end of the animation. This option accepts an object with the `height` and `width` keys which are used to set the ending size of the target element. This option must be supplied
origin	['middle','center']	Sets the vanishing point for hiding animations, or the point from which it grows when used with show logic
scale	"both"	This option sets whether the whole `box` of the element (including border and padding CSS values) is scaled, just the `content`, or as in the default, `both`

Time for action – resizing elements

A popular use of growing and shrinking elements is the Fisheye menu, where elements grow when the mouse pointer hovers over them, and shrink back down when the pointer moves off of them. This effect is also used by the icons on the dock in Apple's OSX.

Using the `size` effect, we can implement our own basic Fisheye menu with just a few lines of code.

1. Add the following markup to the `<body>` of the template file:

```
<div id="dock">
  <a href="#" class="icon" id="finder">
    <img src="img/finder.png"></a>
  <a href="#" class="icon" id="mail">
    <img src="img/mail.png"></a>
  <a href="#" class="icon" id="safari">
    <img src="img/safari.png"></a>
  <a href="#" class="icon" id="firefox">
    <img src="img/firefox_small.png"></a>
  <a href="#" class="icon" id="itunes">
    <img src="img/itunes.png"></a>
</div>
```

2. Add the following JavaScript to the third `<script>` element at the bottom of the `<body>` element:

```
$(".icon", "#dock").hover(function() {
  $(this).stop().animate({
    top: -31
  }).find("img").stop().effect("size", {
  scale: "box", to: { width: 64, height: 64 }
  });
}, function() {
  $(this).stop().animate({
    top: -15
    }).find("img").stop().effect("size", {
    scale: "box", to: { width: 48, height: 48 }
  });
});
```

3. Save this file as `size.html`. We also need some styling. In a new file add the following code:

```
#dock {
  width:380px;
  height:90px;
  position:fixed;
  bottom:0;
  background:url(../img/dock.png) no-repeat 0 0;
}
.icon {
  position:absolute;
```

```
    top:-15px;
    left:44px;
}
.icon img { border:none; }
#mail { left:108px; }
#safari { left:170px; }
#firefox { left:229px; }
#itunes { left:289px; }
```

4. Save this file as `size.css` in the `css` folder.

5. When we run the file in a browser, we should see that the individual items in the menu grow and shrink as the mouse pointer moves over them:

In the previous screenshot we see the menu as the pointer hovers over one of the items in the menu.

What just happened?

We attach the `mouseenter` and `mouseleave` event handlers to each item within the dock using jQuery's `hover()` method, which accepts two functions, the first being executed on the `mouseenter` event, the second being executed on `mouseleave`.

In the first function we use the `stop()` method to manage the queue and then animate the element's position by changing its `top` CSS value. Using `stop()` here prevents an unsightly jarring of the element's position on screen.

We then navigate down the image inside the link and call the `stop()` method on this element, as well, before applying the `size` effect. We provide integer values for the `width` and `height` keys in a configuration object and as these values are larger than the dimensions of the image, the image will be increased in size.

Note that when we use the stop() method with the image, it is to prevent a build-up of effects if the mouse pointer is repeatedly moved on and off one of the links. The second function is really the reverse of the first function, which simply resizes the element back to its original position and size.

The transfer effect

The transfer effect simply transfers the outline of one element to another element. Like the size effect that we looked at a moment ago, the transfer effect will not work if it is not configured.

Syntax

```
$(selector).effect( "transfer", [,configuration] [,duration] );
```

Configuration options

The transfer effect has only two configuration options, although only one of them needs to be set for the effect to work. The configuration options are listed in the following table:

Option	Default	Usage
className	none	The value of this option, if set, is added to the transfer element when the effect runs
to	none	A jQuery selector that specifies the target element that the transfer element is sent to

Time for action – transferring the outline of one element to another

In this example we'll recreate a popular application installation dialog from OSX, and use the transfer effect to help show visitors where to drag the icon (the icon won't actually be draggable; all we're doing is looking at the transfer effect).

1. Add the following elements to the <body> element of the template file to create the install dialog:

```
<div id="install">
  <div id="firefox"></div>
  <div id="apps"></div>
</div>
<p>To install the application, drag its icon over to the apps
folder icon.</p>
<button id="show">Show me</button>
```

2. Add the following script to the empty function at the bottom of the template file:

```
$("#show").click(function() {
  $("#firefox").effect("transfer", {
    to: "#apps",
    className: "ui-effect-transfer"
  }, 1000);
});
```

3. Save the page as `transfer.html`. For the stylesheet add the following code to a new file:

```
body {
    font:normal 14px sans-serif;
}
#install {
  width:417px;
  height:339px;
  position:relative;
  background:url(../img/install.jpg) no-repeat 0 0;
}
#firefox {
  width:124px;
  height:121px;
  position:absolute;
  left:34px;
  top:132px;
  background:url(../img/firefox.png) no-repeat 0 0;
}
#apps {
  width:54px;
  height:52px;
  position:absolute;
  right:58px;
  top:172px;
  background:url(../img/apps.png) no-repeat 0 0;
}
.ui-effect-transfer { border:2px solid #7bee76; }
```

4. Save this file as `transfer.css` in the `css` folder.

5. When the `<button>` element is clicked on, an outline is transferred from the Firefox icon to the App folder icon to direct the visitor:

The transfer element is resized as it moves from the starting element across to the target element. The animation is approximately 50 percent complete in the previous screenshot.

What just happened?

In the underlying HTML we have a container `<div>` element, which is given the background image of the application install dialog box. Within this we have a `<div>` element, which is given the Firefox icon background, and a second `<div>` element, which is given the App folder icon. Both of the inner `<div>` elements are given `id` attributes for styling purposes and for easy selection with jQuery.

In the script we add a click-handler function to the `<button>` element, which applies the effect every time the `<button>` element is clicked. The handler function calls the transfer effect on the `#firefox` element, which sets the icon as the starting element.

In the configuration object, we set the `to` option to a selector for the `apps` element, and the `className` option to the `ui-effect-transfer` string. This string is applied to the element as a class name and is used to add a green border to the transfer element while it is visible.

Each time the `<button>` element is clicked on, the transfer element will be shown and will animate from the starting element (the Firefox icon) to the ending element (the Apps folder icon).

Pop quiz – using the effect API

Q1. How many new effects does jQuery UI give us?

    1. 2

    2. 18

    3. 9

    4. 14

Q2. How is the effect we wish to use specified?

    1. By calling the effect as a function, for example, `bounce()`

    2. The name of the effect is passed in string format to the `effect()` method as the first argument, for example, `effect("bounce")`

    3. The name of the effect is provided as the value of the `effect` key in an object passed to the `animate()` method, for example, `animate({ effect: "bounce" })`

    4. The name of the effect is passed as a string to an event helper, for example, `click("bounce")`

Using effects with the show and hide logic

Some of the jQuery UI effects can also be used in conjunction with jQuery's `show()`, `hide()`, and `toggle()` methods when showing or hiding logic is required. In fact, some of the effects are better suited to this method of execution.

The blind effect

The `blind` effect is the perfect example of an effect that is usually best used with the show/hide logic as opposed to the standard effect API. Although the `blind` effect will work with the standard effect API, what will happen is that the effect will run according to its default mode, but then the element will be put back into its original state. This is true for all effects that have a `mode` configuration option.

Syntax

```
$(selector).hide|show|toggle|effect( "blind", [,configuration]
   [,duration] );
```

Configuration options

The `blind` effect has the following configuration options:

Option	Default	Usage
direction	"vertical"	Sets the axis along which the target element is shown or hidden
mode	"hide"	Sets whether the element is shown or hidden when used with the effect() method. Other possible values include show, toggle, and effect

Time for action – using the blind effect

I mentioned earlier that the effect is reminiscent of a window blind rolling up or down, so let's base our next example on that:

1. In the `<body>` element of the template file add the following code:

```
<div id="window">
    <div id="blind"></div>
</div>
```

2. Implement the effect with the following script:

```
$("#window").click(function() {
  $("#blind").toggle("blind");
});
```

3. Save this file as `blind.html`. The stylesheet for this example is as follows:

```
#window {
  width:464px;
  height:429px;
  position:relative;
  cursor:pointer;
  background:url(../img/window.jpg) no-repeat 0 0;
}
#blind {
  display:none;
  width:332px;
  height:245px;
```

```
   position:absolute;
   left:64px;
   top:113px;
   background:url(../img/blind.png) no-repeat 0 100%;
}
```

4. Save this as `blind.css` in the `css` folder.

5. When we run the page in a browser, the blind should alternately roll down and up each time the window is clicked:

The previous screenshot shows the blind in its fully-open state.

What just happened?

We set a click handler on the outer container which calls the `toggle()` method on the inner element. In the CSS, we set the inner element to be hidden initially, so the first time the container element is clicked, the inner element will be shown.

The clip effect

The `clip` effect causes the element it is called upon to reduce in size vertically or horizontally until it disappears.

Syntax

```
$(selector).hide|show|toggle|effect( "clip", [,configuration]
  [,duration] );
```

Configuration options

The configuration options we have at our disposal when using the `clip` effect allow us to control the direction in which the animation proceeds, and whether the element is shown or hidden:

Option	Default	Usage
direction	"vertical"	Sets the axis along which the element animates
mode	"hide"	Configures whether the element is hidden or shown. Other possible values are show, toggle, and effect

Time for action – clipping an element in and out

This effect is billed as being similar to what happens to the picture when an old television set is turned off, so let's work that into our example.

1. Add the following elements to the `<body>` element of the template file:

```
<div id="tv">
  <div id="bg"></div>
  <div id="static"></div>
</div>
```

2. Then, use the following simple script at the bottom of the page:

```
$("#tv").click(function() {
  $("#static").effect("clip");
});
```

3. Save this file as `clip.html`. The stylesheet for this example is as follows:

```
#tv {
  width:300px;
  height:269px;
  position:relative;
  cursor:pointer;
  background:url(../img/tv.png) no-repeat 0 0;
}
#bg {
```

```
    width:220px;
    height:180px;
    position:absolute;
    left:42px;
    top:30px;
    z-index:-2;
    background-color:#000;
}
#static {
    width:216px;
    height:178px;
    position:absolute;
    left:44px;
    top:31px;
    z-index:-1;
    background:url(../img/static.gif) no-repeat 0 0;
}
```

4. Save this file in the css folder as clip.css.

5. When the page is run, we should be able to click anywhere on the television and see the effect run:

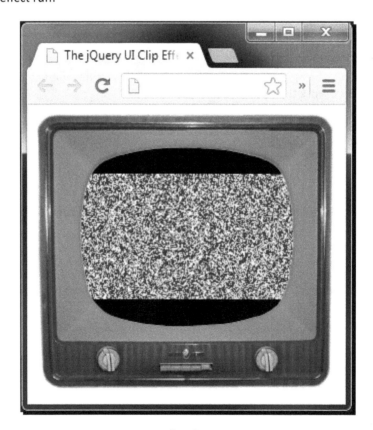

The previous screenshot shows the static element as it is being clipped.

What just happened?

The underlying page has a collection of elements on it with the outer container being styled to look like the television and a couple of inner elements, one of which is a simple background which sits behind the static element. Both inner containers use CSS z-index to sit behind the outer container.

When any part of the television is clicked, the static element has the effect applied to it without any additional configuration, and because the default mode of the effect is hide, the element will be hidden automatically when the effect ends. To see the reverse of the effect, we could hide the static by default and set the mode to show, or we could set the mode to toggle and have the static alternately show and hide.

The drop effect

The drop effect is used to show an element while sliding it open, or hide it while sliding it closed. This effect works on both the position and opacity of the element it is applied to.

Syntax

```
$(selector).hide|show|toggle|effect( "drop", [,configuration]
   [,duration] );
```

Configuration options

The drop effect allows us to control the direction in which the element drops, and whether it is shown or hidden:

Option	Default	Usage
direction	"left"	Sets the direction that the element drops in or out of the page. The other option is the string right
mode	"hide"	Sets whether the element is shown or hidden when using the effect() method. Other possible values include show, toggle, and effect

Time for action – using the effect

The social networking site Twitter introduced a novel effect whereby the system reports actions to the visitor by displaying a message that drops down at the top of the page. We can easily replicate this behavior using the `drop` effect.

1. Add the following markup to the `<body>` element of our template page:

    ```
    <div id="confirmation">
     <p>Your request has been completed!</p>
    </div>
    ```

2. Now, at the bottom of the page add the following code:

    ```
    $("#confirmation").effect("drop", {
      mode: "show",
      direction: "up"
    }, function() {
        var timer = function() {
        $("#confirmation").effect("drop", { mode: "hide",
          direction: "up"});
        }

    setTimeout(timer, 3000);
    });
    ```

3. Save the page as `drop.html`. We only need a few styles for this example. Create the following very basic stylesheet:

    ```
    body { background-color:#3cf; }
    #confirmation {
      display:none;
      width:100%;
      height:60px;
      position:absolute;
      top:0;
      left:0;
      z-index:999;
      background-color:#fff;
      text-align:center;
      font:normal 18px sans-serif;
    }
    #confirmation p {
      margin:0;
      position:relative;
      top:18px;
    }
    ```

4. Save the CSS as `drop.css`.

5. When the page loads, the message should initially be displayed before fading away after a short interval:

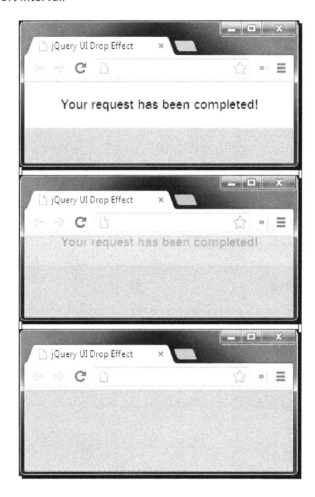

The previous screenshot shows the message slowly being hidden. It will appear to slide up and fade out at the same time when being hidden after the timer interval has passed.

What just happened?

The underlying markup of the message itself is extremely simple; we just need a container and the actual message. In our example the message is hardcoded into the page, but we could easily set this dynamically depending on the action being reported.

The CSS is equally as simple, supplying a background color for the page to better highlight the message, and providing some basic styles for the container and the message itself. The most important rule (in this implementation) is that the container is initially hidden from view.

Our script shows the message as soon as the page has loaded, but normally it would be triggered by the completion of some system action. We use the `effect()` method to initiate the effect and configure the `mode` to `show` and the `direction` to `up` (the element will still appear to drop downwards because it is positioned absolutely) using a configuration object passed as the second argument to the `effect()` method.

Within the callback function passed to the `effect` method, we create an inline function stored in the `timer` variable. Within this function we just hide the confirmation message, using the `effect()` method and setting the `mode` configuration option to `hide` and the `direction` option to `up` once again.

After this function definition, we use JavaScript's `setTimeout` function to execute the `timer` function after 3 seconds have elapsed. We use a closure to call our `timer` function in keeping with the current best practice.

The explode effect

The `explode` effect provides a great visual show by exploding the selected element into a specified number of pieces before fading them away. This effect can be used with both the effect API, as well as the `show`, `hide`, or `toggle` logic.

Syntax

```
$(selector).hide|show|toggle|effect( "explode", [,configuration]
  [,duration] );
```

Configuration options

When using the `explode` effect we can control how many pieces the element is exploded into, and whether the element is shown or hidden:

Option	Default	Usage
mode	"hide"	Sets whether the element is shown or hidden when used with the `effect()` method. Other values are `show`, `effect`, and `toggle`
pieces	9	Sets the number of pieces the element is exploded into

Time for action – exploding an element

In this example we will make an image explode.

1. Just add the following simple image to the `<body>` element of the template file:

   ```
   <img src="img/grenade.jpg" alt="Grenade">
   ```

2. Then add the following equally simple code to the empty function at the bottom of the template file:

   ```
   $("img").click(function() {
     $(this).effect("explode");
   });
   ```

3. Save this page as `explode.html`.

4. This example is so simple we don't even need a stylesheet. Once we click on the grenade, it is exploded into the default number of pieces:

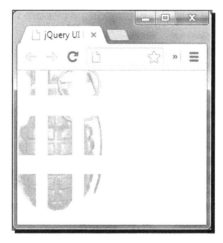

The exploded element fades away as the individual pieces of the element move apart.

What just happened?

In the example, all we need to do is attach a click handler directly to the image which applies the `explode` effect using the `effect()` method. No configuration in this instance is required because the default `mode` of the effect is `hide`.

 Note that we can also run this effect in reverse by setting the `mode` option to `show`, or by using the `show()` logic instead. In this scenario, we will see the target element constructed from a series of pieces that fade in and fly together—an explosion in reverse.

The fold effect

The `fold` effect simulates something being folded in half along one axis and then folded in half along the other axis. Of course, the element isn't actually folded in the 3D sense; first, one side of the element moves up a specified amount, and then another side is moved in and the element disappears.

By default the effect uses the `hide` mode so it will automatically be hidden at the end of the animation. The element being folded is not scaled; it is clipped instead, so images and text will not squash up as the effect runs.

Syntax

```
$(selector).hide|show|toggle|effect( "fold", [,configuration]
  [,duration] );
```

Configuration options

The `fold` effect exposes three configurable options, which are shown in the following table:

Option	Default	Usage
horizFirst	false	Sets whether the element is clipped along the horizontal axis first or not
mode	"hide"	Sets whether the element is shown or hidden when used with the `effect()` method. Other values may include `show`, `effect`, or `toggle`
size	15	This sets the distance of the first fold in pixels and can take either an integer, or a string specifying a value, such as a percentage

Time for action – folding an element away

In this example, we'll apply the fold effect to a simple image of a piece of paper.

1. All we need is an image; add the following code to the `<body>` element of the template file:

```
<img src="img/paper.jpg" alt="A piece of paper">
```

2. Next, add the following simple script to the bottom of the page, in the empty function as with previous examples:

```
$("img").click(function() {
  $(this).effect("fold", { size: "50%" }, 1000);
});
```

3. Save this file as `fold.html`.

4. This is another example that we don't need a stylesheet for. When the image is clicked, it should fold up and disappear:

In the previous screenshots, we see the image first as it starts out, then when the effect has hidden the bottom half of the image, and finally, as the top half of the image is being hidden. Notice that the target element is clipped and not resized.

What just happened?

We simply set a click handler on the `<img>` element, which will apply the `fold` effect. We specify the `size` option as `50%` so that the amount of fold along each axis is equal, and slow the effect down slightly by specifying a longer than default duration of `1000` milliseconds.

The puff effect

The `puff` effect expands the element it is applied to by a specified amount while fading it away to nothing, or fades it in and then shrinks it slightly, depending on how it is used.

Syntax

```
$(selector).hide|show|toggle|effect( "puff", [,configuration]
  [,duration] );
```

Configuration options

The `puff` effect gives us control over the size that the element is increased to, and whether it is shown or hidden:

Option	Default	Usage
mode	"hide"	Sets whether the element is displayed or hidden when used with the `effect()` method. Other possible values include `show`, `effect`, and `toggle`
percent	150	Sets the size the element is scaled to in percent

Time for action – making an element disappear in a puff

In this example, we'll have a dialog box displayed in the center of the browser window and apply the `puff` effect to it when either the **OK** or **Cancel** buttons are clicked.

1. In the `<body>` element of our template file, add the following elements for the dialog:

```
<div id="confirm">
  <img src="img/help.png" alt="Help Icon">
  <p>Are you sure you want to do that?</p>
  <button>Ok</button><button>Cancel</button>
</div>
```

2. Add the accompanying script to the empty function as follows:

```
$("#confirm").css({
  left: $(window).width() / 2 - $("#confirm").width() / 2,
  top: $(window).height() / 2 - $("#confirm").height() / 2
});

$("#confirm, button").click(function() {
  $("#confirm").effect("puff");
});
```

3. Save this page as puff.html. Add the following styles for the dialog box to a new file in your text editor:

```
#confirm {
  display:block;
  width:400px;
  height:120px;
  position:absolute;
  border:1px solid #ccc;
  background:#EEE;
  font:normal 13px sans-serif;
}
#confirm img {
  margin:20px 20px 0 20px;
  float:left;
}
#confirm p { margin:40px 0 0 0; }
#confirm button {
  width:68px;
  margin:20px 10px 0 0;
  float:right;
}
```

4. Save this new file as puff.css in the css directory.

5. When we run the page in a browser, we should find that the dialog is initially centered in the window, and that clicking either of the `<button>` elements closes it using the `puff` effect:

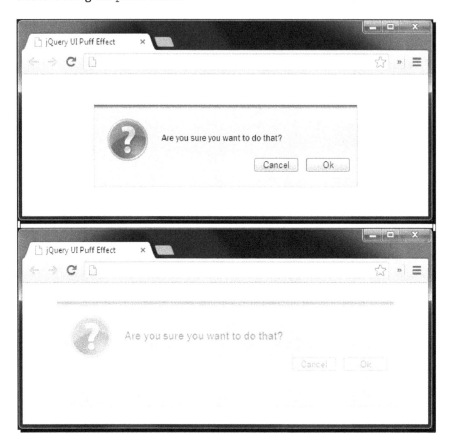

The previous screenshot shows the dialog expanding while it is fading away.

What just happened?

The first part of our script centers the dialog in the window both vertically and horizontally. One point to note is that we cannot use `margin:auto` to center the dialog because it will lose these margins when the effect is applied.

The second part of the script simply adds click handlers to each of the `<button>` elements which apply the `puff` effect when they are clicked on.

The slide effect

The `slide` effect is very similar to the `drop` effect. The only difference is that with the `slide` effect, the opacity of the target element is not adjusted at all. It's also very similar to the slide family of effects exposed by jQuery itself, although with the jQuery UI `slide` effect, we're not restricted to the vertical axis—we can slide horizontally, too.

Syntax

```
$(selector).hide|show|toggle|effect( "slide", [,configuration]
  [,duration] );
```

Configuration options

The `slide` effect has three configuration options which let us specify the direction and distance of the slide, and whether it is shown or hidden:

Option	Default	Usage
direction	"left"	Sets the direction the animation proceeds in
distance	The width of the target element, including padding	Sets the distance that the target element slides to
mode	"show"	Sets whether the element is displayed or hidden when used with the `effect()` method. Other acceptable values are `hide`, `effect`, and `toggle`

Time for action – sliding elements in and out of view

Displaying captions when a visitor hovers over an image is an interactive and interesting way of displaying additional information about the image without making your design appear cluttered. With the `slide` effect, we can easily animate the showing and hiding of the caption, which is what we'll do in this example.

1. Add the following code to the `<body>` element of the template file:

```
<div id="image">
  <img src="img/mantis.jpg" alt="Praying Mantis">
  <div>Praying Mantis: Mantis religiosa</div>
</div>
```

2. Then, at the bottom of the page, in the empty function, add the following short script:

```
$("#image").hover(function() {
  $(this).find("div").stop(true, true).show("slide");
}, function() {
```

```
    $(this).find("div").stop(true, true).hide("slide");
});
```

3. Save this as `slide.html`. Next, create the following stylesheet:

```
#image {
  position:relative;
  float:left;
}
#image img { margin-bottom:-5px; }
#image div {
  display:none;
  width:100%;
  padding:10px 0;
  position:absolute;
  left:0;
  bottom:0;
  top:auto!important;
  text-align:center;
  font-style:italic;
  background-color:#000;
  color:#fff;
}
```

4. Save this file as `slide.css`.

5. When we view the page we should find that the caption is displayed as soon as we move the mouse over the image, and then removed when we move the mouse off of it:

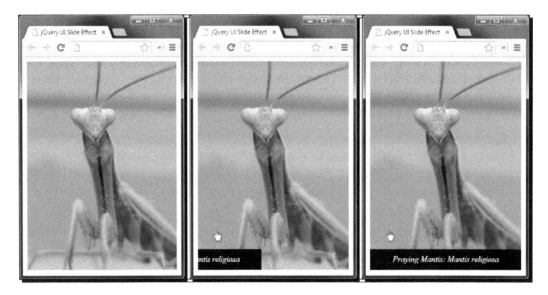

In the previous screenshots we see the caption sliding out from the left edge of the container.

What just happened?

The image and caption are held in a container so that the caption can be positioned accurately. We use jQuery's `hover()` method, which allows us to attach event handlers for both the `mouseover` and `mouseout` events, to show the caption by sliding it in, or hide it by sliding it out.

We don't need any additional configuration in this simple example, but we do need to manage the queue effectively to stop a build-up of animations if the mouse pointer is moved on and off the image repeatedly, which we handle with the `stop()` method.

The scale effect

The `scale` effect is very similar to the `size` effect that we looked at earlier, and as we saw, several effects actually require this effect as a dependency. The main difference between this effect and the `size` effect is that with `scale`, we can only specify a percentage that the target element should be scaled to, not supply exact pixel sizes.

Syntax

```
$(selector).hide|show|toggle|effect( "scale", [,configuration]
  [,duration] );
```

Configuration options

The `scale` effect has more configuration options than any other effect added by jQuery UI.

The configuration options are listed in the following table:

Option	Default	Usage
direction	"both"	Sets which axis the element is scaled along. Other options include `vertical` and `horizontal`
from	none	Sets the starting dimensions of the element
origin	['middle', 'center']	Sets the vanishing point of the element if it is being hidden, or the point from which it grows if it is being shown
percent	0	Sets the percentage by which the element will grow or shrink
scale	"both"	This option sets whether the whole box of the element (including border and padding CSS values) is scaled, just the `content`, or as in the default, `both`

Time for action – scaling an element

It's common practice on an image-heavy site to show a set of thumbnail images which link to a full-sized image that is displayed when the image is clicked, either inline in a modal pop up, or in a separate window. In this example we'll create a thumbnail image that scales to a full-sized version when clicked.

1. Add the following few elements to the `<body>` element of the template file:

```
<div id="container">
  <img src="img/europa.jpg" alt="Europa">
</div>
```

2. The script we need is a little longer, but is still pretty simple. In the empty function at the end of the page, add the following code:

```
$("img").click(function() {
    var img = $(this);

    if(!img.hasClass("full")) {
      img.addClass("full").effect("scale",
        { percent: 400, scale: "box",
        origin: ['top','left'] });
    } else {
      img.removeClass("full").effect("scale",
        { percent: 25, scale: "box",
        origin: ['top','left'] });
    }
});
```

3. Save the page as `scale.html`. In the stylesheet for this example, we'll need the following code:

```
#container {
    position:relative;
    float:left;
    cursor:pointer;
}
#container img {
    width:150px;
    height:150px;
}
```

4. Save this file as `scale.css`.

5. When we run the page we should find that clicking on the image causes it to be scaled up to 400 percent of its initial size:

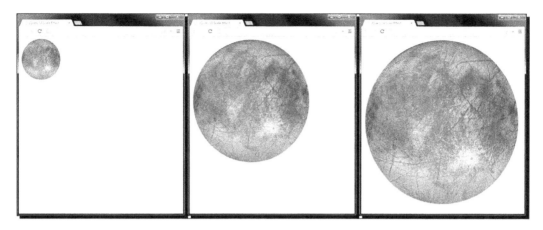

The previous screenshots illustrate the effect in action. Clicking on the image again will scale the image back to its initial state.

What just happened?

On the page our image is held in a simple `<div>` container. The image is scaled down from its original size using CSS, so when we scale the image up we will actually be returning it to full size, so it won't look blocky or fuzzy at all.

In the script we first set a click handler on the image and then cache a reference to it so that we don't have to keep creating jQuery objects referring to this. If the image doesn't have a class name of `full`, we know the image has not been scaled up already, so we add the `full` class and then scale it up by 400 percent using the `percent` option.

Once the image has been scaled, we then create a new anchor element which will be appended to the container element and used as a close button. We set the link's inner text and the `href` attribute, and then assign a click handler to it. Within this handler we prevent the browser following the link and then cache the selector once more, which this time points to the anchor.

We then reduce the image to a quarter of its size, retuning it back to its original dimensions. Once this is done we remove the close link.

Pop quiz – using show/hide logic

Q1. How are supported arguments passed to an effect?

1. In string format as the second argument, for example, `show("blind", "vertical")`

2. As values in a configuration object passed directly to the `animate()` method, for example, `animate({ effect: "blind", configuration: { direction: "vertical" })`

3. As values in a configuration object passed as the second argument, for example, `show("blind", { direction: "vertical" })`

4. By setting the `effect.config` global property, for example, `$.effect.config = { direction: "vertical" })`

Q2. What else can be passed to the method?

1. An integer or string representing the duration, and a callback function or function reference

2. Nothing

3. A Boolean that controls whether the animation should repeat indefinitely

4. A Boolean indicating whether further effects should be queued or executed in parallel

Have a go hero – experimenting with the effect API

I would strongly recommend that you experiment with the effects that we have looked at in this section to see which ones work well with the `effect()` method and which ones work best with the show/hide logic, and so you can see exactly what happens when the ones that don't work so well are used. This should improve your ability to quickly decide exactly when and where each method is appropriate.

Easing functions

Easing can be used with all of the jQuery UI effects with the exception of `explode`, although it can look a little strange in a few of the effects, such as `bounce` or `pulsate`. Easing can also be used if jQuery UI is present with standard jQuery.

Each fading method can have an easing type set by passing an argument into the animation method being used. The sliding animations are the same and can also accept an easing type as an argument. Let's take a moment to familiarize ourselves with what easing is exactly and how it can be used with jQuery animations.

Easing is a technique where the speed and/or the direction of animation are changed while the animation is running. Easing can make the animation start off slow and gradually speed up, start up fast and gradually slow down, and a whole host of other effects.

jQuery has two modes of easing built in: `linear` and `swing`, with `swing` being the default for all types of animations. Sometimes, using the `linear` easing can help make a continuous animation run smoother, but the difference between `swing` and `linear` is subtle at best.

 Animated demos of all of the easing types can be viewed by going to the following URL:

http://api.jqueryui.com/easings.

The easing types of jQuery UI add-ins are listed in the following table:

easeInQuad	easeOutQuad	easeInOutQuad
easeInCubic	easeOutCubic	easeInOutCubic
easeInQuart	easeOutQuart	easeInOutQuart
easeInQuint	easeOutQuint	easeInOutQuint
easeInExpo	easeOutExpo	easeInOutExpo
easeInSine	easeOutSine	easeInOutSine
easeInCirc	easeOutCirc	easeInOutCirc
easeInElastic	easeOutElastic	easeInOutElastic
easeInBack	easeOutBack	easeInOutBack
easeInBounce	easeOutBounce	easeInOutBounce

Time for action – adding easing to effects

To use easing, all we need to do is include the easing function name as a configuration option. For example, to add easing to the `blind.html` example that we looked at earlier, we could change the JavaScript so that it appeared as follows:

```
$("#window").click(function() {
    $("#blind").toggle("blind", { easing: "easeOutBounce" });
});
```

What just happened?

We use the configuration option, `easing`, with the name of the easing function as a string supplied as the value of the option. Any of the easing functions can be used by referencing their name in this way.

Using an object literal to add easing

We can also change the format of the arguments we pass into the predefined animation methods in order to use easing. Prior to the easing argument being added to the animation methods (`fadeIn()`, `slideDown()`, and so on) in version 1.4.3 of jQuery, this was the defacto means of using easing with animation methods.

Instead of providing string or numerical arguments (or a callback function), we can provide an object literal where each key refers to the duration, the easing type, and optionally a callback to call when the animation is complete. The usage then becomes as follows:

```
$(elements).toggle("blind", {
  duration: [duration],
  easing: [easing],
  complete: [callback]
});
```

Have a go hero – using easing

Try out some of the other easing methods on some of our earlier examples. We'll be using easing wherever appropriate throughout the remainder of the book, but other than a cursory explanation these won't be focused on in any great detail.

Pop quiz – using easing

Q1. How many easing types are there in total?

1. 20
2. 32
3. 17
4. 48

Q2. What can we pass into an `effect()` method in the alternative format for using easing?

1. An object with optional keys specifying the duration, easing type, and a function to call on complete
2. A string specifying the easing type
3. An array where the first item is the duration, the second is the easing type, and the third is a function to call on complete
4. An integer specifying the duration of easing

Animating between different colors

As well as the complete range of easing functions, the `effects` core file also gives us the ability to attractively and smoothly animate between different colors. Several CSS properties can be animated, including the `color`, `background-color`, `border-color`, and `outlinecolor`.

jQuery UI extends jQuery's `animate()` method to achieve color animations, so the syntax to implement it is the same as using `animate()`. For any other purpose, we just need to target one of the above CSS properties and supply a valid color value (hexadecimal, RGB/RGBa, HSL, and so on). Let's look at a basic example.

Time for action – animating between colors

In this example, we'll use color animations to show that a form field has been left empty.

1. In a fresh copy of the template file, use the following elements in the `<body>` of the page:

```
<input><button id="search">Search</button>
```

2. To invoke the color changes when the `<button>` is clicked, we can use the following JavaScript in the empty function near the bottom of the document:

```
$("#search").click(function (e) {
  e.preventDefault();

  var input = $(this).prev();

  if (input.val() == "") {
    input.animate({
      backgroundColor: "#f78080",
      borderColor: "#a72b2e"}, 1200);
  };
});
```

3. Save this page as `color-animations.html`. We literally only need a couple of styles for this example. We could probably get away with defining them in a `<style>` block in the `<head>` element of the page. We just use the following CSS:

```
input {
  width:200px;
  border:2px solid #27659f;
}
```

4. When we run the page, we see that the text field changes color if the `<button>` element is clicked on while it is empty.

What just happened?

The CSS, while extremely small, is required in this example because the `<input>` field will lose any attractive styling provided by modern browsers when the colors are animated. Setting the CSS properties we are animating helps prevent this ugly switch.

In the script we simply cache a selector that points to the `<input>` field, and then test whether the field is empty. If it is, we call the `animate()` method, specifying the aspects of the target element we'd like to animate.

Class transitions

As well as extending jQuery's `animate()` method in order to provide color animations, jQuery UI also extends some of jQuery's element manipulation methods. The following methods are extended to provide class transitions:

◆ `addClass()`

◆ `removeClass()`

◆ `toggleClass()`

jQuery UI also exposes a new method for transitioning between two classes: the `switchClass()` method, which accepts the current class and new class, as well as duration, easing, and callback arguments.

Time for action – transitioning between classes

We can rework our previous example so that it uses some of the class transition methods.

1. Add the class name `default` to the `<input>` element and then change the JavaScript so that it appears as follows:

```
$("#search").click(function(e) {
  e.preventDefault();

  var input = $(this).prev();

  if (input.val() == "") {
    input.switchClass("default", "error", 1200);
  } else if (input.val() && input.hasClass("error")) {
    input.removeClass("error", 1200);
  }
});
```

2. Save the new page as `class-animation.html`. We'll need to make some changes to the stylesheet as well. Create a new stylesheet and add the following rules to it (or change the styles in the `<head>` element of the page):

```
input { width:200px; }
input, .default { border:2px solid #27659f; }
.error {
  border:2px solid #a72b2e;
  background-color:#f78080;
}
```

3. Save the new file as `class-animation.css`.

4. Run the page in a browser and again, click the `<button>` element without entering anything into the text field. The `<input>` field should transition to the `error` class and appear the same as it did in the last example. This time, however, enter some text in the `<input>` field and click the `<button>` element again. The error should then transition back to default.

What just happened?

This time, if the `<input>` field has no value, we just call the `switchClass()` method, specifying the current class of default, the new class of `error`, and a duration of `1.2` seconds. Note that you must supply both the current and new classes for the example to work correctly.

In the next branch of the conditional, we check that the `<input>` field has both a value and a class name of `error`. If it does, we call the `removeClass()` method specifying just the class to remove and a duration. The duration is required in order to trigger the transition.

In the CSS we provide the default styling using the class name `default` as well as generally for all of the `<input>` fields. We need to do this because otherwise the element loses its styles while the `error` class is in the process of being removed, causing it to revert to a standard, unstyled `<input>` field.

Performance: When using jQuery, it's generally best that we change the class name of an element rather than manipulating an element's `style` attribute directly. Because of this, it's natural to assume that using `switchClass()` would be more efficient than using `animate()`.

This, however, is not the case, as Firebug's profile tool will show. In the previous example, if the second branch of the conditional is removed and the page and both `color-animation.html` and `class-animation.html` are profiled, it is `color-animation.html` that wins by a margin of around 20 milliseconds.

Pop quiz – easing, color, and class animations

Q1. How are easing functions specified?

1. In string format as the third argument to the `effect()` method, for example, `effect("blind", {}, "easeOutBounce")`

2. As Boolean in a callback function, for example, `effect("blind", function() { easeOutBounce = true })`

3. Easing cannot be used

4. In string format as the value of the easing configuration option, for example, `effect("blind", { easing: "easeOutBounce" })`

Q2. Which method is extended to produce color animations?

1. The `effect()` method

2. The `show()` method

3. The `animate()` method

4. The `switchClass()` method

Summary

In this chapter we looked at the complete range of effects that are added by the jQuery UI library. We looked at how they can be used with the `effect()` method, or the `show()`, `hide()`, and `toggle()` methods when necessary. We saw the configuration arguments that each effect takes, and their default values when used out of the box.

We also covered how jQuery UI extends the `animation()`, `addClass()`, and `removeClass()` methods, and the `switchClass()` method that it adds in order to add the ability to animate between colors and classes.

The key points to take from this chapter include:

♦ jQuery UI together with jQuery can be downloaded using the jQuery UI download builder, which builds a custom package, complete with a theme if required for you to download.

♦ jQuery UI adds a total of 14 new, predefined effects to our animation toolkit. The effects are easy to use, but highly configurable.

♦ The `effect()` method is the basic means of specifying an effect, its configuration options, a duration, and a callback function.

- Some of the effects work much better with the `show()`, `hide()`, or `toggle()` methods, and are equally as easy to use with this aspect of the API.

- The easing functions are built directly into jQuery UI and can be used by specifying them as values for the `easing` configuration option.

- jQuery UI also gives us the ability to transition an element's color or class name by extending some of jQuery's methods and adding the new `switchClass()` method.

In the next chapter, we'll switch back to jQuery and look at custom animations, including custom transitions, a custom-made slideshow, animating an element's dimensions, and how to create a jQuery animation plugin.

7
Custom Animations

The predefined effects that we have looked at throughout the book so far are very good at what they do, but they are there to cater to very specific requirements and will sometimes not be enough when more complex animations are needed.

In these situations, we can use jQuery's animate() *method, which allows us to easily define custom animations that can be as complex and as specialized as the task at hand requires. This is what we'll be looking at over the course of this chapter.*

Subjects that we'll cover throughout the course of this chapter include:

- ◆ Creating custom animations with the animate() method
- ◆ Passing arguments to the method
- ◆ Animating an element's dimensions
- ◆ Animating an element's position
- ◆ Creating a jQuery animation plugin
- ◆ Using the jQuery plugin we created

The animate method

All custom animations with jQuery are driven by the animate() method. Despite the ability to animate almost any style property that has a numeric value, this method is simple to use and takes just a few arguments. This method may be used in the following way:

```
$(elements).animate( properties [,duration] [,easing] [,complete] );
```

The first argument should take the form of an object, where each property of the object is a style that we'd like to animate, very similar to how we would use jQuery's `css()` method.

As I mentioned before, this can be any CSS style that takes a purely numerical argument (with the exception of colors, although with the jQuery UI library, we can animate colors as well. See *Chapter 6, Extended Animations with jQuery UI*, for more information on jQuery UI). Background positions cannot be animated by jQuery natively, but it is quite easy to animate this property manually; see *Chapter 3, Background Animation*, for more information on this technique.

The duration, easing, and callback arguments take the same formats as those that we used with the fading methods earlier in the book (*Chapter 2, Image Animation*) and are used in exactly the same way.

Per-property easing

As of jQuery Version 1.4, you can set per-property easing functions within a single `animate()` call. So, for example, if we are animating both the `width` and `height` parameters of an element, we can use the `linear` easing for the `width` animation, and the `swing` easing for the `height` animation. This applies to the standard easing functions built into jQuery, or any of the easing functions we talked about in the previous chapter (*Chapter 6, Extended Animations with jQuery UI*).

To supply easing types to the `animate()` method on a per-property basis, we need to provide an array as the value of the property we are animating. This can be done using the following syntax:

```
$(elements).animate({
  property: [value, easingType]
});
```

An alternative syntax for animate()

Instead of using the duration, easing, and callback arguments individually, we may alternatively pass a configuration object to the `animate()` method containing the following configuration options:

- `duration`
- `easing`
- `complete`
- `step`
- `queue`
- `specialEasing`

The first three options (`duration`, `easing`, and `complete`) are the same as the arguments would be if we passed them into the method in the standard way. The last three options (`step`, `queue`, and `specialEasing`) are interesting, however, in that we do not have access to them in any other way.

- The `step` option allows us to specify a callback function that will be executed on each step of the animation

- The `queue` option accepts a Boolean value that controls whether the animation is executed immediately or placed into the selected element's queue

- The `specialEasing` option allows us to specify an easing function for each individual style property that is being animated, giving us easing on a per-property basis using the alternative syntax:

  ```
  The pattern for this second method of usage is as
  follows:$(elements).animate(properties [,configuration]);
  ```

Like most (but not all) jQuery methods, the `animate()` method returns a jQuery object so that additional methods can be chained to it. Like the other effect methods, multiple calls to `animate()` on the same element will result in an animation queue being created for the element. If we want to animate two different style properties at the same time, we can pass all of the required properties within the object passed to the `animate()` method as the first argument.

Animating an element's position

The `animate()` method is able to animate changes made to any CSS style property that has a numeric value, with the exception of colors and background positions. In this example, we'll create a content viewer that shows different panels of content by sliding them in and out of view using the `animate()` method.

This type of widget is commonly used on portfolio or showcase sites and is an attractive way to show a lot of content without cluttering a single page. In this example, we'll be animating the element's position.

Time for action – creating an animated content viewer

We'll start again by adding the underlying markup and styling:

1. The underlying markup for the content viewer should be added as follows using our template file:

```
<div id="slider">
  <div id="viewer">
    <img id="image1" src="img/amstrad.jpg" alt="Amstrad CPC 472">
    <img id="image2" src="img/atari.jpg" alt="Atari TT030">
    <img id="image3" src="img/commodore16.jpg" alt="Commodore 64">
    <img id="image4" src="img/commodore128.jpg" alt="Commodore
      128">
    <img id="image5" src="img/spectrum.jpg" alt="Sinclair ZX
      Spectrum +2">
  </div>
  <ul id="ui">
    <li class="hidden" id="prev">
      <a href="" title="Previous">«</a></li>
    <li><a href="#image1" title="Image 1" class="active">Image
      1</a></li>
    <li><a href="#image2" title="Image 2">Image 2</a></li>
    <li><a href="#image3" title="Image 3">Image 3</a></li>
    <li><a href="#image4" title="Image 4">Image 4</a></li>
    <li><a href="#image5" title="Image 5">Image 5</a></li>
    <li class="hidden" id="next">
      <a href="" title="Next">»</a></li>
  </ul>
</div>
```

2. Save the file as `animate-position.html`.

3. Next, we should create the base CSS. By that, I mean we should add the CSS that is essential for the content viewer to function as intended, as opposed to styling that gives the widget a theme or skin. It's a good practice to separate out the styling in this way when creating plugins so that the widget is compatible with jQuery UI's ThemeRoller theming mechanism.

4. In a new file in your text editor, add the following code:

```
#slider {
  width:500px;
  position:relative;
}
#viewer {
  width:400px;
```

```
    height:300px;
    margin:auto;
    position:relative;
    overflow:hidden;
}
#slider ul {
    width:295px;
    margin:0 auto;
    padding:0;
    list-style-type:none;
}
#slider ul:after {
    content:".";
    visibility:hidden;
    display:block;
    height:0;
    clear:both;
}
#slider li {
    margin-right:10px;
    float:left;
}
#prev, #next {
    position:absolute;
    top:175px;
}
#prev { left:20px; }
#next {
    right:10px;
}
.hidden { display:none; }
#slide {
    width:2000px;
    height:300px;
    position:absolute;
    top:0;
    left:0;
}
#slide img { float:left; }
#title {
    margin:0;
    text-align:center;
}
```

5. Save this in the css folder as `animate-position.css`, and don't forget to link to the new stylesheet from the `<head>` tag of our page. Run the page in your browser now before we get into the scripting, so that you can see how the widget behaves without the accompanying script. You should find that any image can be viewed by clicking on its corresponding link using only CSS, and this will work in any browser. The previous and next arrows are hidden with our CSS because these will simply not work with JS turned off and when the image titles are not displayed, however, the widget's core functionality is still fully accessible. This is known as **progressive enhancement** and is considered by many to be the best practice for web development.

What just happened?

The underlying HTML in this example is very straightforward. We have an outer container for the content-viewer as a whole, and then within this, we have a container for our content panels (simple images in this example), and a navigation structure to allow the different panels to be viewed.

Some of the elements we've added style rules for in our CSS file aren't hardcoded into the underlying markup, but will be created as necessary when needed. Doing it this way ensures that the content-viewer is still usable even when the visitor has JavaScript disabled.

One important point to note is that the `#slide` wrapper element that we created and wrapped around the images has a `height` parameter equal to a single image and a `width` parameter equal to the sum of all image widths. The `#viewer` element, on the other hand, has both a `width` and a `height` parameter equal to a single image, so that only one image is visible at any one time.

With JavaScript disabled, the images will appear to stack up on top of each other, but once the `#slide` wrapper element has been created, the images are set to float in order to stack up horizontally.

We'll use easing in this example; so be sure to link to jQuery UI directly after the jQuery reference at the end of the `<body>` tag:

```
<script src="js/jquery-ui.js"></script>
```

Time for action – initializing variables and prepping the widget

First, we need to prepare the underlying markup and store some element selectors. Add the following code between our anonymous function in our newly created HTML file:

```
$("#viewer").wrapInner("<div id=\"slide\"></div>");

var container = $("#slider"),
  prev = container.find("#prev"),
```

```
      prevChild = prev.find("a"),
      next = container.find("#next").removeClass("hidden"),
      nextChild = next.find("a"),
      slide = container.find("#slide"),
      key = "image1",
      details = {
        image1: {
          position: 0, title: slide.children().eq(0).attr("alt")
        },
        image2: {
          position: -400, title: slide.children().eq(1).attr("alt")
        },
        image3: {
          position: -800, title: slide.children().eq(2).attr("alt")
        },
        image4: {
          position: -1200, title: slide.children().eq(3).attr("alt")
        },
        image5: {
          position: -1600, title: slide.children().eq(4).attr("alt")
        }
      };

  $("<h2>", {
    id: "title",
    text: details[key].title
  }).prependTo("#slider");
```

What just happened?

To start with, we first wrapped all of the images inside `#viewer` in a new container. We'll be using this container to animate the movement of the panels. We give this new container an `id` attribute so that we can easily select it from the **Document Object Model** (**DOM**) when required.

This is the element that we will be animating later in the example.

Next, we cache the selectors for some of the elements that we'll need to manipulate frequently. We create a single jQuery object pointing to the outer `#slider` container and then select all of the elements we want to cache, such as the previous and next arrows, using the jQuery `find()` method.

A `key` variable is also initialized, which will be used to keep track of the panel currently being displayed. Finally, we create a `details` object that contains information about each image in the content viewer. We can store the `left` position in pixels that the `slide` container must be animated to in order to show any given panel, and we can also store the title of each content panel.

The title of each panel is read from the `alt` attribute of each image, but if we were using other elements, we could select the `title` attribute, or use jQuery's data method to set and retrieve the title of the content.

The `<h2>` element used for the title is created and inserted into the content-viewer with JS because there is no way for us to change it without using JavaScript. Therefore, when visitors have JS disabled, the title is useless and is better off not being shown at all.

The last thing we do in the first section of code is to remove the `hidden` class name from the next button so that it is displayed.

The previous link (by this, I mean the link that allows the visitor to move to the previous image in the sequence) is not shown initially, because the first content panel is always the panel that is visible when the page loads, so there are no previous panels to move to.

Time for action – defining a post-animation callback

Next, we need a function that we can execute each time an animation ends. Add the following code beneath the code we added previously:

```
function postAnim(dir) {

  var keyMatch = parseInt(key.match(/\d+$/));

  (parseInt(slide.css("left")) < 0) ? prev.show() : prev.hide();

  (parseInt(slide.css("left")) === -1600) ? next.hide() :
    next.show();

  if (dir) {
    var titleKey = (dir === "back") ? keyMatch - 1 : keyMatch + 1;
    key = "image" + titleKey;
  }

  container.find("#title").text(details[key].title);

  container.find(".active").removeClass("active");
  container.find("a[href=#" + key + "]").addClass("active");
};
```

What just happened?

In this second section of the code, we define a function that we'll call after an animation ends. This is used for some housekeeping to do various things that may need to be done repeatedly; so, it is more efficient to bundle them up into a single function instead of defining them separately within event handlers. This is the `postAnim()` function, and it may accept a single parameter which refers to the direction that the slider has moved in.

The first thing we do in this function is use the regular expression, `/\d+$/`, with the JavaScript's `match()` function to parse the panel number from the end of the string saved in the `key` variable, which we initialized in the first section of code, and which will always refer to the currently visible panel.

Our `postAnim()` function may be called either when a panel is selected using the numeric links, or when the previous/next links are used. However, when the previous/next links are used, we need the `key` variable to know which panel is currently being displayed in order to move to the next or previous panel.

We then check whether the first panel is currently being displayed by checking the `left` CSS style property of the `#slide` element. If the `#slide` element is at `0`, we know the first panel is visible, so we hide the previous link. If the `left` property is less than `0`, we show the previous link. We do a similar test to check whether the last panel is visible, and if so, we hide the next link. The previous and next links will only be shown if they are currently hidden.

We then check whether the `dir` (direction) argument has been supplied to the function. If it has, we have to work out which panel is now being displayed by reading the `keyMatch` variable that we created earlier, and then either subtract `1` from it if the `dir` argument is equal to `back`, or add `1` to it, if not.

The result is saved back to the `key` variable, which is then used to update the `<h2>` title element. The title text for the current panel is obtained from our `details` object using the `key` variable. Lastly, we add the class name `active` to the numeric link corresponding to the visible panel.

Although not essential, this is something we will want to use when we come to add a skin to the widget. We select the right link using an attribute selector that matches the `href` attribute of the current link. Note that we don't create any new jQuery objects in this function; we use our cached `container` object and the `find()` method to obtain the elements we require.

Time for action – adding event handlers for the UI elements

Now that the slider has been created, we can add the event handlers that will drive the functionality. Insert the following code beneath the postAnim function we just added in:

```
$("#ui li a").not(prevChild).not(nextChild).click(function(e){
  e.preventDefault();

  key = $(this).attr("href").split("#")[1];

  slide.animate({
    left: details[key].position
  }, "slow", "easeOutBack", postAnim);
});

nextChild.add(prevChild).click(function(e){
  e.preventDefault();

  var arrow = $(this).parent();

  if (!slide.is(":animated")) {
    slide.animate({
      left: (arrow.attr("id") === "prev") ? "+=400" : "-=400"
    }, "slow", "easeOutBack", function(){

      (arrow.attr("id") === "prev") ? postAnim("back") :
        postAnim("forward")
    });
  }
});
```

What just happened?

The first handler is bound to the main links used to display different panels, excluding the previous and next links with the jQuery not() method. We first stop the browser following the link with the preventDefault() method.

We then update the key variable with the panel that is being displayed by extracting the panel name from the link's href attribute. We use JavaScript's split() method to obtain just the panel id and not the # symbol.

Finally, we animate the slide element by setting its `left` CSS style property to the value extracted from the `details` object. We use the `key` variable to access the value of the `position` property.

As part of the animation, we configure the duration as `slow` and the easing as `easeOutBack`, and specify our `postAnim` function as the callback function to execute when the animation ends.

Finally, we need to add a click handler for the previous/next links used to navigate to the next or previous image. These two links can share a single-click handler. We can select both of these two links using our cached selectors from earlier `nextChild` and `prevChild`, along with jQuery's `add()` method, to add them both to a single jQuery object in order to attach the handler functions to both links.

We again stop the browser from following the link using `preventDefault()`. We then cache a reference to the parent of the link that was clicked, using the `arrow` variable, so that we can easily refer to it later on in the function. This is needed because within the callback function for the `animate()` method, the `$(this)` keyword will be scoped to the `#slide` element instead of the link that was clicked.

We then check that the `#slide` element is not already being animated using the `:animated` filter. This check is important because it prevents the viewer from breaking if one of the links is clicked repeatedly.

If it is not already being animated, we perform the animation and move the slide element either `400` pixels (the `width` parameter of a single content panel) backward or forward. We can check which arrow was clicked by looking at the `id` attribute of the element referenced by the `arrow` variable.

We specify the same duration and easing values as before in the animation method, but instead of passing a reference to the `postAnim` function as the callback parameter, we pass an anonymous function instead. Within this anonymous function, we determine which link was clicked and then call the `postAnim` function with the appropriate argument. Remember, this is necessary to obtain the correct key for the `details` object, because neither the previous nor the next links have the `href` attributes pointing to an image.

Try the page out in a browser at this point and you should find that an image can be viewed by clicking on any of the links, including the previous and next links. This is how the widget should appear at this stage:

The previous screenshot shows the widget in its un-skinned state, with only the JavaScript required for it to function.

Skinning the widget

"There's more than one way to skin a cat", was once proclaimed, and this applies to widgets, as well as cats. Lastly, let's add some custom styling to the widget to see how easy it is to make the widget attractive, as well as functional. These styles can easily be changed to re-skin the widget to give it a completely different look.

Time for action – adding a new skin

At the bottom of the `animate-position.css` file, add the following code:

```
a { outline:0 none; }
#slider {
```

```
    border:1px solid #999;
    -moz-border-radius:8px;
    -webkit-border-radius:8px;
    border-radius:8px;
    background-color:#ededed;
    -moz-box-shadow:0 2px 7px #aaa;
    -webkit-box-shadow:0 2px 7px #aaa;
    box-shadow:0 2px 7px #aaa;
}
#title, #slider ul {
    margin-top:10px;
    margin-bottom:12px;
}
#title {
    font:normal 22px "Nimbus Sans L", "Helvetica Neue",
    "Franklin Gothic Medium", Sans-serif;
    color:#444;
}
#viewer {
    border:1px solid #999;
    background-color:#fff;
}
#slider ul { width:120px; }
#slider ul li a {
    display:block;
    width:10px;
    height:10px;
    text-indent:-5000px;
    text-decoration:none;
    border:2px solid #666;
    -moz-border-radius:17px;
    -webkit-border-radius:17px;
    border-radius:17px;
    background-color:#fff;
    text-align:center;
}
#slider #prev, #slider #next {
    margin:0;
    text-align:center;
}
#slider #prev { left:10px; }
#slider #prev a, #slider #next a {
    display:block;
    height:28px;
    width:28px;
    line-height:22px;
    text-indent:0;
    border:1px solid #666;
    -moz-border-radius:17px;
    -webkit-border-radius:17px;
```

```
    border-radius:17px;
    background-color:#fff;
}
#prev a, #next a {
    font:bold 40px "Trebuchet MS", sans-serif;
    color:#666;
}
#slider ul li a.active { background-color:#F93; }
```

What just happened?

With this code, we style all of the visual aspects of the widget without interfering with anything that controls its working. We give it some nice rounded corners and add a drop-shadow to the widget, turn the numeric links into little clickable icons, and style the previous and next links. Colors and fonts are also set in this section as they, too, are obviously highly dependent on the theme.

These styles add a basic, neutral theme to the widget, as shown in the following screenshot:

The styles we used to create the theme are purely arbitrary and simply for the purpose of the example. They can be changed to whatever we need in any given implementation to suit other elements on the page, or the overall theme of the site.

Pop quiz – creating an animated content-viewer

Q1. What arguments may the `animate()` method pass?

1. An array where the array items are the element to animate, the duration, the easing, and a callback function

2. The first argument is an object containing the style properties to animate, optionally followed by the duration, an easing type, and a callback function

3. An object where each property refers to the style properties to animate, the duration, easing, and a callback function

4. A function which must return the style properties to animate, the duration, easing, and a callback function

Q2. What does the `animate()` method return?

1. An array containing the style properties that were animated

2. A array containing the elements that were animated

3. A jQuery object for chaining purposes

4. A Boolean indicating whether the animation completed successfully

Have a go hero – making the image viewer more scalable

In our animated content-viewer, we had a fixed number of images and a hardcoded navigation structure to access them. Extend the content viewer so that it will work with an indeterminate number of images. To do this, you will need to complete the following tasks:

◆ Determine the number of images in the content-viewer at runtime and set the `width` parameter of the `#slide` wrapper element based on the number of images

◆ Build the navigation links dynamically based on the number of images

◆ Create the `details` object dynamically based on the number of images, and set the correct `left` properties to show each image

Animating an element's size

As mentioned at the start of the chapter, almost any style property that contains a purely numeric value may be animated with the `animate()` method.

We looked at animating an element's position by manipulating its `left` style property, so let's move on to look at animating an element's size by manipulating its `height` and `width` style properties.

In this example, we'll create image wrappers that can be used to display larger versions of any images on the page by manipulating the element's size.

Time for action – creating the underlying page and basic styling

First, we'll create the underlying page on which the example will run.

1. Add the following HTML to the `<body>` tag of our template file:

```
<article>
  <h1>The Article Title</h1>
  <p><img id="image1-thumb" class="expander" alt="An ASCII
    Zebra" src="img/ascii.gif" width="150" height="100">Lorem
    ipsum dolor...</p>
  <p><img id="image2-thumb" class="expander" alt="An ASCII
    Zebra" src="img/ascii2.gif" width="100" height="100">Lorem
    ipsum dolor...</p>
</article>
```

2. Save the example page as `animate-size.html`. We'll keep the styling light in this example; in a new file in your text editor, add the following code:

```
article {
  display:block;
  width:800px;
  margin:auto;
  z-index:0;
  font:normal 18px "Nimbus Sans L", "Helvetica Neue",
    "Franklin Gothic Medium", sans-serif;
}
article p {
  margin:0 0 20px;
  width:800px;
  font:15px Verdana, sans-serif;
  line-height:20px;
}
article p #image2-thumb {
  float:right;
  margin:6px 0 0 30px;
}
img.expander {
  margin:6px 30px 1px 0;
  float:left;
}
.expander-wrapper {
  position:absolute;
```

```
    z-index:999;
  }
  .expander-wrapper img {
    cursor:pointer;
    margin:0;
    position:absolute;
  }
  .expander-wrapper .expanded { z-index:9999; }
```

3. Save this file as `animate-size.css` in the `css` folder.

What just happened?

The HTML could be any simple blog post consisting of some text and a couple of images. The points to note are that each image is given an `id` attribute so that it can be easily referenced, and that each image is actually the full-sized version of the image, scaled down with the `width` and `height` attributes.

The styles used are purely to lay out the example; very little of the code is actually required to make the example work. The `expander-wrapper` styles are needed to position the overlaid images correctly, but other than that, the styling is purely arbitrary.

We're floating the second image to the right. Again, this isn't strictly necessary; it's used just to make the example a little more interesting.

Time for action – defining the full and small sizes of the images

First, we need to specify the full and small sizes of each image. Place the following code into our anonymous function inside the HTML file we just created:

```
var dims = {
  image1: {
    small: { width: 150, height: 100 },
    big: { width: 600, height: 400 }
  },
  image2: {
    small: { width: 100, height: 100 },
    big: { width: 400, height: 400 }
  }
},
webkit = ($("body").css("-webkit-appearance") !== "" && $("body").
css("-webkit-appearance") !== undefined) ? true : false;
```

What just happened?

We created an object which contains properties matching each image's filename. Each property contains another nested object, which has the `small` and `big` properties and the relevant integers as values. This is a convenient way to store structured information that can easily be accessed at different points in our script.

We also created a variable called `webkit`. There is a slight bug in how images floated to the right are treated in WebKit-based browsers. This variable will hold a Boolean that will indicate whether WebKit is in use.

A test is performed which tries to read the `-webkit-appearance` CSS property. In WebKit browsers, the test will return `none`, as the property is not set, but other browsers will either return an empty string or the value `undefined`.

Time for action – creating the overlay images

Next, we should create an almost exact copy of each image on the page to use as an overlay. Add the following code beneath the code we just added to our HTML file:

```
$(".expander").each(function(i) {

  var expander = $(this),
    coords = expander.offset(),
    copy = $("<img>", {
      id: expander.attr("id").split("-")[0],
      src: expander.attr("src"),
      width: expander.width(),
      height: expander.height()
    });
```

What just happened?

In this part of the `<script>` tag, we selected each image on the page and processed them using jQuery's `each()` method. We set some variables, caching a reference to the current image, and storing its coordinates on the page relative to the document using the jQuery `offset()` method.

We then create a new image for each existing image on the page, giving it an `id` attribute that pairs it with the image it is overlaying, the `src` variable of the original image, and the `width` and `height` parameters of the original image. We use JavaScript's `split()` function to remove the part of the string that says `thumb` when we set the `id` attribute of the new image.

Note that the previous code does not represent an entire snippet of fully-functional code. The outer function passed to the each() method has not yet been closed, as we need to add some additional code after these variables.

Time for action – creating the overlay wrappers

We now need to create the wrappers for each of the overlay images (note that this code is still within the each() method, and so will be executed for each of the images that have the expanded class name). Add the following code directly below the last line of the each function we just added:

```
$("<div></div>", {
  "class": "expander-wrapper",
  css: {
    top: coords.top,
    left: (webkit === true && expander.css("float") === "right") ?
      (coords.left + expander.width()) : coords.left,
      direction: (expander.css("float") === "right") ? "rtl" :
      "ltr"
  },
  html: copy,
  width: expander.width(),
  height: expander.height(),
  click: function() {

    var img = $(this).find("img"),
      id = img.attr("id");

    if (!img.hasClass("expanded")) {
      img.addClass("expanded").animate({
        width: dims[id].big.width,
        height: dims[id].big.height
      }, {
        queue: false
      });
    } else {
      img.animate({
        width: dims[id].small.width,
        height: dims[id].small.height
      }, {
```

```
            queue: false,
            complete: function() {
               $(this).removeClass("expanded");
            }
         });
      }
   }
}).appendTo("body");
```

What just happened?

In this section of code, we create the wrapper element for the new image. We give it a new class name so that it can be positioned correctly.

Quoting the class property

We need to use quotes around the property name `class` because it's a reserved word in JavaScript and could throw script errors if this isn't done.

We set the position of the wrapper element using the `css` property, in conjunction with the coordinates we obtained from the `offset()` method earlier.

When setting the `left` position of the wrapper element, we need to check our `webkit` variable to see if Safari or Chrome is in use. If this variable is set to `true`, and if the image is floated to the right, we position the overlay according to the `cords.left` value, in addition to the `width` parameter of the original image. If the `webkit` variable is `false`, or if the original image is floated `left`, we just set the `left` position of the wrapper to the value stored in `coords.left`.

We also need to set the `direction` property of any images that are floated right. We check the `float` style property and set the `direction` to `rtl` if the image is floated right, or `ltr` if not. This is done using JavaScript, a ternary conditional.

This check is done so that the wrapper expands from right to left when the image is floated `right`. If we didn't set this, the wrapper would open up from left to right, which could make the full-sized image overflow the viewport, or the content container result in scroll bars.

We add the new image to the wrapper by passing a reference to it into the jQuery `html()` method, and set the `width` parameter of the wrapper to the `width` parameter of the original (and new) image. This is necessary for the overlay to be positioned correctly over any images that are floated right.

Next, we add a click handler to the wrapper. Within the anonymous function passed as the value of the `click()` method, we first cache a reference to the image within the wrapper that was clicked, and get the `id` attribute of the image for convenience. Remember, the `id` attribute of the overlay image will be the same as the original image it is covering, minus the text string `-thumb`.

We then check whether the image has the class name `expanded`. If it doesn't, we add the class name and then animate the image to its full size using the second format of the `animate()` method. We pass two objects into the method as arguments; the first contains the CSS properties we wish to animate, in this case, the `width` and `height` parameters of the image.

The correct `width` and `height` parameters to increase the image are retrieved from the `dims` object using the `id` attribute of the image that was clicked as the key. In the second object passed to the `animate()` method, we set the `queue` property to `false`. This has the same effect as using the `stop()` method directly before the `animate()` method and ensures that nothing bad happens if the overlay wrapper is repeatedly clicked.

If the image already has the class name `expanded`, we animate the image back to its small size. Again, we use the two-object format of the `animate()` method, supplying `false` as the value of the `queue` property, and removing the class name `expanded` in an anonymous callback function passed to the `complete` property. Once the wrapper has been created, we append it to the `<body>` tag of the page.

At this point, the code we've written will work as intended—clicking on an image will result in the expanded version being animated to its full size. However, if the page is resized at all, the overlays will no longer be overlaying their images.

Time for action – maintaining the overlay positions

Because the overlays are positioned absolutely, we need to prevent them from becoming misaligned if the window is resized:

```
$(window).resize(function() {

  $("div.expander-wrapper").each(function(i) {

    var newCoords = $("#image" + (i + 1) + "-thumb").offset();

    $(this).css({
      top: newCoords.top,
      left: newCoords.left
    });
  });
});
```

What just happened?

All we need to do is make sure the overlay images stay directly on top of the original images when the page resizes, which we can achieve by binding a handler for the resize event to the `window` object. In the handler function, we just get the new coordinates of the underlying image, and set the `top` and `left` properties of the wrapper accordingly. Note that we don't animate the repositioning of the overlays.

Save the file and preview it in your browser. We should find that we can click on either image and it will expand to show a full-sized version of the image, with the first image expanding to the right and the second expanding to the left:

In the previous screenshot we see the first image as it expands to its full size.

Pop quiz – creating expanding images

Q1. In this example, we used a different format for the arguments passed to the `animate()` method. What format did the arguments take?

1. Two arrays where the first array contains selectors for the elements to animate and the second contains the duration, easing, the `specialEasing` strings, and a callback function

2. A single object containing the style properties to animate, duration, easing, and the `specialEasing` strings, and `step` and `complete` callback functions

3. A function which must return the style properties to animate, the duration and easing strings, and a callback function

4. Two objects where the first object contains the style properties to animate, and the second object contains the duration, easing and the `specialEasing` strings, a Boolean indicating whether to queue repeated `animate()` calls, and the step and complete callback functions

Q2. What is the keyword `this` scoped to in an animation's callback function?

1. The element that was animated

2. The current window

3. The container of the element that was animated

4. The event object

Have a go hero – doing away with the hardcoded dims object

In the previous example, we hardcoded an image into the top of our script that was used to tell the `animate()` method what size the image should be animated to. While this was fine for the purpose of the example, it doesn't really scale well as a long-term solution as we would have to remember to set this every time we used the script (or otherwise ensure our images are always of a fixed size).

The problem is that we have no way to programmatically get both the full size and thumb size from a single image. The good news is that any data that can be stored in a JavaScript object can also be passed across a network for consumption as a JSON object. Extend this example so that when the page loads, it passes the `src` attributes of the images on the page to the server, which returns a JSON object containing the small and large image sizes. An image manipulation library, such as GD or ImageMagick, for PHP, ImageResizer, or the `System.Drawing.Image` type in .NET, will be your friend here.

Creating a jQuery animation plugin

Plugins are an excellent way of packaging up functionality into an easy-to-deploy and share module of code that serves a specific purpose. jQuery provides the `fn.extend()` method precisely for this purpose, making it easy to create powerful and effective plugins that can be easily distributed and used.

There are a few guidelines that should be adhered to when creating jQuery plugins. These are as follows:

- New methods, which are called like other jQuery methods, for example, `$(elements).newMethod()`, should be attached to the `fn` object, and new functions, which are used by the plugin, for example, `$.myFunction()`, should be attached to the `jQuery` object

- New methods and functions should always end in a semi-colon (`;`) to preserve the functionality when the plugin is compressed

- Inside methods, the `this` keyword always refers to the current selection of elements, and methods should always return `this` to preserve chaining

- Always attach new methods and functions to the `jQuery` object, as opposed to the `$` alias, unless using an anonymous function with an aliased `$` object

In this section, we'll create a plugin that can be used to create advanced transition effects when showing a series of images. The finished widget will be similar in some respects to the image viewer we created earlier, but will not animate the images themselves. Instead, it will apply transition effects between displaying them.

Time for action – creating a test page and adding some styling

Once again, we'll create the example page and basic styling first and add the script last.

1. The underlying HTML for this example is very light. All we need in the `<body>` tag of our template file are the following elements:

```html
<div id="frame">
    <img class="visible" src="img/F-35_Lightning.jpg" alt="F-35
      Lightning">
    <img src="img/A-12_Blackbird.jpg" alt="A-12 Blackbird">
    <img src="img/B-2_Spirit.jpg" alt="B-2 Spirit">
    <img src="img/SR-71_Blackbird.jpg" alt="SR-71 Blackbird">
    <img src="img/F-117_Nighthawk.jpg" alt="F-117 Nighthawk">
</div>
```

2. Save this page as `advanced-transitions.html`.

3. Like the markup, the CSS we rely on for a plugin should also be as minimal as possible. Luckily, not much CSS is required for our small collection of elements.

4. Add the following code to a new file in your text editor:

```
#frame {
  position:relative;
  width:520px;
  height:400px;
  z-index:0;
}
#frame img {
  position:absolute;
  top:0;
  left:0;
  z-index:1;
}
#frame img.visible { z-index:2; }
#frame a {
  display:block;
  width:50%;
  height:100%;
  position:absolute;
  top:0;
  z-index:10;
  color:transparent;
  background-image:url(transparent.gif);
  filter:alpha(opacity = 0);
  text-align:center;
  text-decoration:none;
  font:90px "Palatino Linotype", "Book Antiqua",
    Palatino, serif;
  line-height:400%;
}
#frame a:hover {
  color:#fff;
  text-shadow:0 0 5px #000;
  filter:alpha(opacity=100);
  filter:Shadow(Color=#000, Direction=0);
}
#frame a:focus { outline:none; }
#prev { left:0; }
#next { right:0; }
#overlay {
  width:100%;
```

```
    height:100%;
    position:absolute;
    left:0;
    top:0;
    z-index:3;
}
#overlay div { position:absolute; }
```

5. Save this in the `css` folder as `advanced-transitions.css`.

What just happened?

All we have on the underlying page are the images between which we wish to make transition within a container. It's best to keep the markup requirements for plugins as simple as possible so that they are easy for others to use and don't place undue restrictions on the elements or structure they want to use.

The images are positioned absolutely within the container using CSS so that they stack up on top of one another, and we set our `visible` class on the first element to ensure one image is above the rest in the stack.

Most of the styling goes towards the previous and next anchors, which we'll create with the plugin. These are set so that each one will take up exactly half of the container and are positioned to appear side-by-side. We set the `z-index` property of these links so that they appear above all of the images. The `font-size` property is ramped up considerably, and an excessive `line-height` means we don't need to middle-align the text with `padding`.

In most browsers, we simply set the `color` property of the anchors to `transparent`, which hides them. Then, we set the `color` property to white in the `hover` state. This won't work too well in IE, however, so instead we set the link initially to transparent with the Microsoft `opacity filter`, and then set it to fully opaque in the `hover` state, which serves the same purpose.

Another IE-specific fix

IE also presents us with another problem: the clickable area of our links will only extend the height of the text within them because of their absolute positioning. We can overcome this by setting a reference to a background image.

The best part is that the image doesn't even need to exist for the fix to work (so you'll find no corresponding `transparent.gif` file in the book's companion code bundle). The fix has no detrimental effects on normal browsers.

Creating the plugin

Now, let's create the plugin itself. Unlike most of the other example code we've looked at, the code for our plugin will go into its own separate file.

Time for action – adding a license and defining configurable options

In a new file, create the following outer structure for the plugin and save it in our `js` folder under the name `jquery.tranzify.js`:

```
/*
  Plugin name jQuery plugin version 1.0

  Copyright (c) date copyright holder

  License(s)

*/

;(function($) {

  $.tranzify = {

    defaults: {
      transitionWidth: 40,
      transitionHeight: "100%",
      containerID: "overlay",
      transitionType: "venetian",
      prevID: "prev",
      nextID: "next",
      visibleClass: "visible"
    }
  };

})(jQuery);
```

What just happened?

All plugins should contain information on the plugin name, version number, the copyright owner (usually the author of the code), and the terms, or links to the terms, of the license or licenses it is released under.

The plugin is encapsulated within an anonymous function so that its variables are protected from other code which may be in use on the page it is deployed on. It also has a semicolon placed before it to ensure it remains a discrete block of code after potential minification, and in case it is used with other less scrupulously written code than our own.

We also alias the $ character for safe use within our function, to ensure it is not hijacked by any other libraries running on the page, and to preserve the functionality of jQuery's noConflict() method.

It is a good practice to make plugins as configurable as possible so that end users can adjust them to suit their own requirements. To facilitate this, we should provide a set of default values for any configurable options. When deciding what to make configurable, a good rule of thumb is to hardcode nothing other than pure logic into the plugin. Hence, IDs, class names, and anything like that should be made configurable.

The defaults we set for the plugin are stored in an object that is itself stored as a property of the jQuery object that is passed into the function. The property added to the jQuery object is called tranzify, the name of our plugin, and will be used to store the properties, functions, and methods we create so that all of our code is within a single namespace.

Our default properties are contained in a separate object, called defaults, within the tranzify object. We set the width and height parameters of the transition elements, the id attribute of the container that gets created, the default transition, the id attributes for the previous and next links, and the class name we give to the currently displayed image.

As I mentioned, it's best not to hardcode any id values or class names into a plugin if possible. The person implementing the plugin may already have an element on the page with an id attribute of overlay, for example, so we should give them the option to change it if need be.

Time for action – adding our plugin method to the jQuery namespace

Next, we can add the code that will insert our plugin into the jQuery namespace so that it can be called like other jQuery methods. Add the following code directly above the last line in the code we just added:

```
$.fn.extend({
  tranzify: function(userConfig) {

    var config = (userConfig) ? $.extend({}, $.tranzify.defaults,
      userConfig) : $.tranzify.defaults;

    config.selector = "#" + this.attr("id");
```

```
        config.multi = parseInt(this.width()) / config.transitionWidth;

        $.tranzify.createUI(config);

        return this;
    }
});
```

What just happened?

jQuery provides the `fn.extend()` method specifically for adding new methods that can
be chained to the `jQuery()` function, which is how most plugins are created. We defined a
function as the value of the sole property of an object passed to the `extend()` method. We
also specified that the method may take one argument, which may be a configuration object
passed into the method by whoever is using the plugin to change the default properties
we set.

The first thing our method does is check whether or not a configuration object has been
passed into the method. If it has, we use the `extend()` method (not `fn.extend()`,
however) to merge the user's configuration object with our own `defaults` object.

The resulting object, created by the merging of these two objects, is stored in the variable
`config` for easy access by our functions. Any properties that are in the `userConfig`
object will overwrite the properties stored in our `defaults` object. Properties found
in the `defaults` object but not the `userConfig` object will be preserved. If no
`userConfig` object is passed into the method, we simply assign the `defaults`
object to the `config` variable.

Next, we built an `id` selector that matched the element of the method that was called on
and added this as an extra property to the `config` object, making it convenient to use
throughout the plugin. We can't store this as a default property because it is likely to be
different on every page that the plugin is used on, and we also can't expect users of the
plugin to have to define this in a configuration object each time the plugin is used.

The number of transition elements we need to create will depend on the size of the images
and the width of the transition elements (defined as a configurable property), so we worked
out a quick multiplier based on the width of the image and then configured transition width
for use later on.

Following this, we called the function that will create the previous/next links (we will define
this shortly) and passed the function, the `config` object, so that it can read any properties
that the user has configured.

Finally, we return the jQuery object (which is automatically assigned to the value of the `this` keyword within our plugin method). This is to preserve chaining so that the user can call additional jQuery methods after calling our plugin.

Time for action – creating the UI

Next, we need to create the previous and next links that are overlaid above the images and allow the visitor to cycle through the images. Add the following chunk of code beneath the `$.fn.extend()` section we just added:

```
$.tranzify.createUI = function(config) {
  var imgLength = $(config.selector).find("img").length,
    prevA = $("<a></a>", {
    id: config.prevID,
    href: "#",
    html: "«",
    click: function(e) {
      e.preventDefault();

      $(config.selector).find("a").css("display", "none");

      $.tranzify.createOverlay(config);

      var currImg = $("." + config.visibleClass, $(config.selector));
      if(currImg.prev().filter("img").length > 0) {
        currImg.removeClass(config.visibleClass).prev().addClass
          (config.visibleClass);
      } else {
        currImg.removeClass(config.visibleClass);
        $(config.selector).find("img").eq(imgLength -
          1).addClass(config.visibleClass);
      }

      $.tranzify.runTransition(config);

    }
  }).appendTo(config.selector),

  nextA = $("<a></a>", {
    id: config.nextID,
    href: "#",
    html: "»",
    click: function(e) {
      e.preventDefault();
```

```
        $(config.selector).find("a").css("display", "none");

        $.tranzify.createOverlay(config);

        var currImg = $("." + config.visibleClass, $(config.selector));

        if(currImg.next().filter("img").length > 0) {
          currImg.removeClass(config.visibleClass).next().addClass(
            config.visibleClass);
        } else {
          currImg.removeClass(config.visibleClass);
          $(config.selector).find("img").eq(0).addClass(
            config.visibleClass);
        }

        $.tranzify.runTransition(config);
      }
    }).appendTo(config.selector);
  };
```

What just happened?

This is by far our largest function and deals with creating the previous and next links, as well as defining their click handlers during the creation using the jQuery syntax. The first thing we do is obtain the number of images in the container, as the click handlers we add will need to know this.

We create the anchor for the previous link, and in the object passed as the second argument, we define the id attribute (using the value from the config object), a dummy href, an HTML entity as its innerHTML, and a click handler.

Within the click handler, we use the preventDefault() method to stop the browser following the link, then hide the previous and next links in order to protect the widget against multiple clicks, as this will break the transitions.

Next, we call our createOverlay() function, passing it the config object, to create the overlay container and the transition elements. We also cache a reference to the currently selected image using the class name stored in the config object.

We then test whether there is another image element before the visible image. If there is, we remove the class from the element that currently has it and give it to the previous image in order to bring it to the top of the stack. If there aren't any more images before the current image, we remove the visible class from the current image and move to the last image in the container to show that instead.

Once we've defined everything we need, we can append the new anchor to the specified container. We also create the next link within the current function, as well, giving it a very similar set of attributes and a click handler, too. All that differs in this click handler is that we test for an image after the current one, and move to the first image in the container if there isn't one.

Time for action – creating the transition overlay

Our next function will deal with creating the overlay and transition elements:

```
$.tranzify.createOverlay = function(config) {

  var posLeftMarker = 0,
    bgHorizMarker = 0

  overlay = $("<div></div>", {
    id: config.containerID
  });

  for (var x = 0; x < config.multi; x++) {

    $("<div></div>", {
      width: config.transitionWidth,
      height: config.transitionHeight,
      css: {
        backgroundImage: "url(" + $("." + config.visibleClass,
          $(config.selector)).attr("src") + ")",
        backgroundPosition: bgHorizMarker + "px 0",
        left: posLeftMarker,
        top: 0
      }
    }).appendTo(overlay);
      bgHorizMarker -=config.transitionWidth;
    posLeftMarker +=config.transitionWidth;

  }
  overlay.insertBefore("#" + config.prevID);
};
```

What just happened?

Our previous function dealt with creating the overlay container and the transition elements that will provide the transition animations. The plugin will need to set the `position` and `background-position` properties of each transition element differently in order to stack the elements up horizontally. We'll need a couple of counter variables to do this, so we initialize them at the start of the function.

We then create the overlay container `<div>` and give it just an `id` attribute, so that we can easily select it when we run the transitions.

Next, we create the transition elements. To do this, we use a standard JavaScript `for` loop, which is executed a number of times depending on the multiplier we set earlier in the script. On each iteration of the loop, we create a new `<div>`, which has its `width` and `height` parameters set according to the properties stored in the configuration object.

We use the `css()` method to set the `backgroundImage` property of the overlay to the currently visible image, and the `backgroundPosition` property according to the current value of the `bgHorizMarker` counter variable. We also set the `left` property to position the new element correctly according to the `posLeftMarker` variable, and the `top` property to `0` to ensure correct positioning.

Once created, we append the new element to the container and increment our counter variables. Once the loop exits and we have created and appended all of the transition elements to the container, we can then append the container to the element on the page that the method was called on.

Time for action – defining the transitions

The final function will perform the actual transitions:

```
$.tranzify.runTransition = function(config) {
  var transOverlay = $("#" + config.containerID),
    transEls = transOverlay.children(),
    len = transEls.length - 1;

  switch(config.transitionType) {
    case "venetian":
    transEls.each(function(i) {
      transEls.eq(i).animate({
        width: 0
      }, "slow", function() {

        if (i === len) {
          transOverlay.remove();
```

```
            $(config.selector).find("a").css("display", "block");
          }
        });
      });
      break;
      case "strip":
      var counter = 0;

    function strip() {
      transEls.eq(counter).animate({
        height: 0
      }, 150, function() {

        if (counter === len) {
          transOverlay.remove();
          $(config.selector).find("a").css("display", "block");
        } else {
          counter++;
          strip();
        }
      });
    }
    strip();
  }
};
```

What just happened?

Our last function deals with actually running the transitions. In this example, there are just two different types of transitions, but we could easily extend this to add more transition effects.

This function also requires some variables, so we set these at the start of the function for later use. We cache a reference to the overlay container, as we'll be referring to it several times. We also store the collection of transition elements and the number of transition elements. We subtract 1 from the number of children because the figure will be used with the jQuery's `eq()` method, which is zero-based.

To determine which of our transitions to run, we use JavaScript's `switch` statement and check the value of the `config.transitionType` property. The first transition is a kind of **venetian-blind** effect. To run this transition, we just animate the `width` parameter of each element to 0 using jQuery's `each()` method. The function we specify as the argument to this method automatically receives the index of the current element, which we access using `i`.

In the callback function for each animation, we check whether i is equal to the `length` of the collection of transition elements, and if it is, we remove the overlay and show the previous and next links once more.

The second transition removes the old image one strip at a time. To do this, we use a simple `counter` variable and a standard JavaScript function. We can't use the `each()` method this time, or all of the transition elements will slide down together, but we want each one to slide down on its own.

Within the function, we animate the current transition element's height to 0 and set a rather low duration so that it happens fairly quickly. If the animation is too slow, it spoils the effect. In the callback function, we check whether our `counter` variable is equal to the number of transition elements, and if so, remove the overlay and show the links again. If the `counter` variable hasn't reached the last element at this point, we increment the `counter` variable and call the function once more.

Save this file as `jquery.tranzify.js` in the `js` folder. This is the standard naming convention for jQuery plugins and should be adhered to.

Using the plugin

To use the plugin, we just call it like we would call any other jQuery method, inside our ready function or anonymous function, like the following:

```
<script>
  $(function() {
    $("#frame").tranzify();
  });
</script>
```

In this form, the default properties will be used. If we want to change one of the properties, we just supply a configuration object, such as this:

```
$("#frame").tranzify({
  transitionType: "strip"
});
```

The default animation should run something like this:

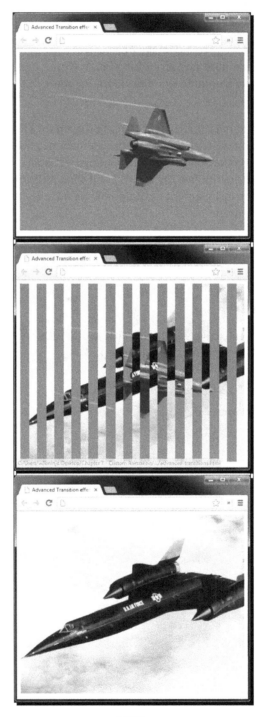

In the previous screenshot, we see the transition elements all simultaneously shrinking to 0 width, creating an effect like Venetian blinds being opened to reveal the new image.

Using the plugin is simple; there is just one point to remember. All of the images should be of same size, and the width parameter of each image should be exactly divisible by the transitionWidth property. As we've exposed the transitionWidth property as a configurable property, we should be able to use an image of any size we wish and set this accordingly.

For reference, the second transition effect runs like this, with strips of the old image sliding away to reveal the new image:

In the previous screenshot, we can see the effects of the second transition type, with the old image being stripped away to reveal the new image.

Pop quiz – creating a plugin

Q1. What is the difference between a plugin method and a function?

1. There is no difference, conceptually and in practice they are the same

2. Methods are able to accept arguments, functions are not

3. Methods execute faster

4. Methods are attached to the `fn` object and are used like existing jQuery methods, while functions are attached directly to the jQuery object and called like any normal function

Q2. What must each new method return?

1. A string containing the `id` attribute of the selected element

2. An array containing the `id` attributes of selected elements

3. The `this` object, which points to the currently selected element

4. Nothing should be returned

Have a go hero – extending the plugin

Our plugin currently contains just two transition effects (venetian and strip). Extend the plugin to include more transition effects of your own devising. The plugin currently creates a number of transition elements that are the full height of each image.

By wrapping our existing `for` loop within another `for` loop and adding some new counter variables for `top` position and vertical `background-position`, it is relatively easy to add square transition elements in a checkerboard style, which opens up the possibility of more complex and attractive transition effects. Do this.

Summary

In this chapter, we looked at some common usages of the `animate()` method, which is the means for us to create custom animations in jQuery when the built-in effects are not enough for our requirements. The method is robust, easy to use, and makes complex animations trivial.

When simple sliding or fading does not meet our requirements, we can fall back onto the `animate()` method in order to craft our own high-quality custom animations. We learned the following points about the `animate()` method:

- The `animate()` method can be used to animate any numeric CSS property (except colors, for which jQuery UI is required).

- The arguments passed into the method may take one of two formats. The first allows us to pass an object containing the CSS properties to animate, as well as separate duration, easing, and callback arguments. The second format allows us to pass in two objects, the first allowing us to specify the CSS properties to animate as before, and the second allowing us to specify additional options, such as the duration, easing, and callback. The second option gives us access to some special arguments not accessible in the first format, such as `specialEasing` and the `step` callback.

- All CSS properties specified in the first object will be executed simultaneously.

- How to achieve animations involving an element's position, or its dimensions

We also looked at how we can extend the jQuery library with brand new functions and methods in the form of plugins. Plugins are a great way of wrapping up code for easy deployment and sharing.

Now that we've looked at all of jQuery's animation methods, in the next chapter, we're going to take a look at other popular animations, such as adding mouse and keyboard events and animating the post links.

8
Other Popular Animations

This chapter will follow a similar format to the previous one and will consist of a series of recipe-style examples that show the real-world implementations of animations in action. We won't restrain ourselves—anything goes!

We'll look at the following examples in this chapter:

- Proximity animations, where the animation is a reaction to the proximity of the mouse pointer to a target element or area of the page
- An animated header element
- A text-scrolling marquee widget

Understanding Proximity animations

Proximity animations, which are usually driven by the position of the mouse pointer relative to an element or series of elements on the page, are an awesome effect. While not suitable on all sites and in all contexts, it can add real flair when used in certain situations.

The effect isn't often very accessible, and pretty much shuts the door on non-mouse users, but it can be implemented as an additional bonus (often called progressive enhancement) to visitors that are able to make use of it, while at the same time providing other, more accessible forms of interaction.

In this example, we'll create an image scroller that is triggered when the mouse pointer enters its container. The speed with which the images will scroll will be determined by the distance of the mouse pointer from the center of the container. Moving the pointer will slow down or speed up the animation accordingly.

Time for action – creating and styling the page

In this part of the example we'll create the underlying page that the animation will run on, and add the styling.

1. First, we'll create the default page, and add the CSS for the example. Add the following elements to the `<body>` element of our template file:

```
<div id="proximity">
  <img src="img/proximity1.jpg" alt="CH-47 Chinook">
  <img src="img/proximity2.jpg" alt="Mi-24W">
  <img src="img/proximity3.jpg" alt="Mil Mi-24A">
  <img src="img/proximity4.jpg" alt="AH-1J Cobra">
  <img src="img/proximity5.jpg" alt="Mi-24P">
  <img src="img/proximity6.jpg" alt="AH-1Z Viper">
  <img src="img/proximity7.jpg" alt="AH-1W Cobra">
  <img src="img/proximity8.jpg" alt="UH-1Y Huey">
  <img src="img/proximity9.jpg" alt="AH-64 Apache">
  <img src="img/proximity10.jpg" alt="AH-1W Super Cobra">
  <img src="img/proximity11.jpg" alt="MI-28 Havoc">
  <img src="img/proximity12.jpg" alt="AH-1W Super Cobra">
  <img src="img/proximity13.jpg" alt="AH-1W Cobra">
  <img src="img/proximity14.jpg" alt="Mi-24 HIND E">
  <img src="img/proximity15.jpg" alt="AH-1W Super Cobra">
  <img src="img/proximity16.jpg" alt="UH-1N Huey">
  <img src="img/proximity17.jpg" alt="AH-64D Apache">
  <img src="img/proximity18.jpg" alt="UH-1N Huey">
  <img src="img/proximity19.jpg" alt=" Lempira Bell 412">
  <img src="img/proximity20.jpg" alt="UH-60L Blackhawk">
</div>
```

2. Save this file as `proximity.html`. Next, we'll add some CSS. In a new file, add the following code:

```
/* base classes (scripting disabled) */
#proximity {
  width:960px;
  margin:auto;
  border:1px solid #000;
  -moz-border-radius:8px;
  -webkit-border-radius:8px;
  border-radius:8px;
}
#proximity img { border:1px solid #000; }
```

```
/* scripting enabled classes */
#proximity.slider {
  width:550px;
  height:250px;
  position:relative;
  overflow:hidden;
}
.slider #scroller {
  position:absolute;
  left:0;
  top:0;
}
.slider #scroller img {
  display:block;
  width:150px;
  height:150px;
  margin:50px 0 0 50px;
  float:left;
  color:#fff;
  background-color:#000;
}
.slider #scroller img:first-child { margin-left:0; }
#message {
  width:100%;
  height:30px;
  padding-top:10px;
  margin:0;
  -moz-border-radius:0 0 8px 8px;
  -webkit-border-bottom-radius:8px;
  -webkit-border-bottom-right-radius:8px;
  border-radius:0 0 8px 8px;
  position:absolute;
  bottom:0;
  left:0;
  background-color:#000;
  color:#fff;
  text-align:center;
  font:18px "Nimbus Sans L", "Helvetica Neue",
    "Franklin Gothic Medium", Sans-serif;
}
```

3. Save this in the css folder as `proximity.css` and don't forget to link to it from the `<head>` of the HTML page.

What just happened?

Keeping the HTML as simple and as light as possible, we simply add the images that we want to show to a container element. Any extra elements that we need can be added dynamically in the nature of progressive enhancement.

There are two sections in the CSS file. The first section is a collection of base styles which are used if the page is loaded by a visitor that has JavaScript disabled. This ensures that all of the images are visible and therefore accessible—none of them are hidden or otherwise obscured.

The second section changes the appearance of the container element and adds styling to elements or classes that are added dynamically, transforming the appearance of the slider, provided JavaScript is enabled.

We set the `height` and `width` of the container so that only three images are visible at any one time, and set its `overflow` style property to `hidden` so that all of the other images are hidden, ready to be scrolled into view.

We also add positioning for an element with an `id` of `scroller`. This element doesn't yet exist and will be added by the script, which we'll look at shortly. This element will also need a `width`, but we can assign this dynamically based on the number of images in the container.

We also change the styling of the images themselves, setting them to block-level elements and floating them to the left so that they stack up horizontally in a long line, without wrapping onto two lines as this would destroy the functionality of the scroller. It is the combination of floating the images and setting the `width` of the container to accommodate them all, that allows them to stack up as horizontally as required. We'll add a message that tells the visitor how to use the scroller so we also include some styling for this, as well.

The following screenshot shows how the page will appear with scripting disabled:

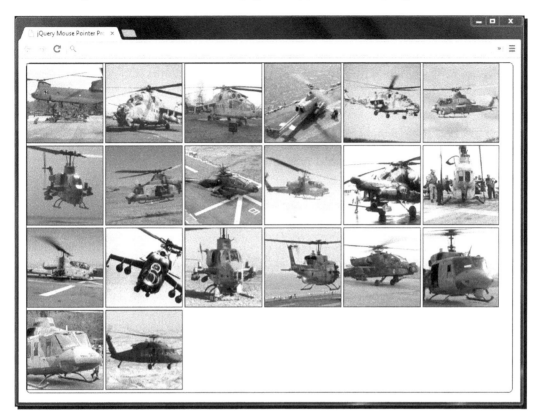

In the previous image we can see that the images are all visible. It's not pretty, but it's highly accessible and doesn't hide the content when scripting is disabled on the client.

Time for action – preparing the page for sliding functionality

When scripting is enabled, we can enhance the page to add the additional elements that the proximity slider requires. Add the following code to the empty function at the bottom of the HTML page:

```
var prox = $("#proximity"),
  scroller = $("<div></div>", {
    id: "scroller"
  }),

  pointerText = "Use your pointer to scroll, moving to "+
    "the edge scrolls faster!",
  keyboardMessage = "Use your arrow keys to scroll the images!",
  message = $("<p></p>", {
```

```
      id: "message",
      text: keyboardMessage
   });

prox.addClass("slider").wrapInner(scroller).append(message);

var middle = prox.width() / 2;

scroller = $("#scroller");

scroller.width(function() {
   var total = 0;
   scroller.children().each(function(i, val) {
      var el = $(this);
      total = total + (el.outerWidth() +
         parseInt(el.css("marginLeft")));
});
return total;

}).css("left", "-" + (scroller.width() / 2 - middle) + "px");
```

What just happened?

First, we cache the selector for the proximity container, which we'll use a couple of times in this chunk of code, and a couple of times a little later on in the script. Next, we create a new <div> element and give it an id attribute so that we can easily select it again when necessary. We also use this id for styling purposes.

Next, we store a couple of text strings in variables for convenience. These will be used as messages to display to the visitor at different points. We also create a new paragraph element as a container for the message text, give the element an ID (again for selecting purposes), and use the jQuery text() method to set its innerText to one of the text strings. We then use the property text on the object passed as the second argument to the element creation jQuery method format, which automatically maps to the text() method.

Next, we add a class name to the outer proximity container. Remember, this class name is used to differentiate between scripting being disabled and enabled so that we can add the required styling. We also wrap the contents of the proximity container (the 20 <img> tags) in our newly created scroller element, and append the message to the proximity container.

Next, we set a variable which is equal to the width of the proximity container divided by two. This gives us the horizontal middle of the element, which we'll need to use in some calculations to position the scroller element, and work out where the mouse pointer is relative to the proximity container.

We could just as easily have set the number that the middle variable needs to contain, instead of calculating it in this way. The width of the proximity container (with scripting enabled) is set in our CSS file and is highly arbitrary to this particular example. If we changed its width however, the script would break if we set the figure directly in the variable instead of working it out programmatically. It is always best to avoid hardcoding 'magic' numbers into scripts whenever possible.

At this point we also need to cache a reference to the scroller element now that it has been appended to the page. We can't use the contents of the scroller variable that we created at the start of the script, so we overwrite it with a fresh reference to the element by selecting it from the page again.

We now need to set the width of the scroller element so that it is wide enough to accommodate all of the images in a single row. To do this we pass a function to jQuery's width() method, which returns the width to be set.

The function calculates this figure by iterating over each image and adding both its width and horizontal margin to the total variable. This means that an indeterminate number of images can be used without changing the script, and images with different widths and spacing can be used.

Once we've set the width of the scroller element, we then need to position it so that the center of the scroller is at the center of the proximity container. This is so that when the page loads, the visitor can move it to the left or right, depending on where they move their pointer or which arrow key is pressed.

If we load the page in a browser at this point, we should find that the appearance of the elements on the page has changed.

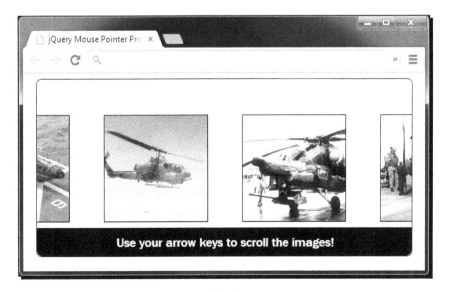

In the previous screenshot, we can see that the proximity container is resized and the `scroller` element is centered within it. We can also see the default message at the bottom of the proximity container.

Time for action – animating the scroller

The next section of code deals with actually animating the `scroller` element based on where the mouse pointer is relative to the outer proximity container. Add the following code below the `}).css("left", "-" + (scroller.width()` line:

```
function goAnim(e) {

  var offset = prox.offset(),
    resetOffset = e.pageX - offset.left - middle,

    normalizedDuration = (resetOffset > 0) ? resetOffset :
      -resetOffset,

    duration = (middle - normalizedDuration) * 50;

    scroller.stop().animate({
      left: (resetOffset < 0) ? 0 : "-" + (parseInt(scroller.width())
        - parseInt(prox.width()))
    }, duration, "linear");
}
```

What just happened?

Within the `goAnim()` function, we first get the `offset` value of the proximity container so that we know its position relative to the document. We then work out where the mouse pointer is relative to the middle of the proximity container. This means that numerically, the pointer offset will be `0` when it is in the center.

If the mouse pointer is in the left half of the proximity container, the number in the `resetOffset` variable will be negative. This would cause our calculations later in the function to be incorrect, so we need to check whether the `resetOffset` variable is greater than `0`, and if it isn't, we invert the number using its minus value.

Ultimately, what we want to happen is for the speed of the scroller to increase as the pointer moves towards either end of the proximity container, and slow down as it moves into the center. In other words, the speed of the animation needs to be inversely proportionate to the distance of the pointer from the middle of the proximity container.

The problem that we have at this point is that the figure representing the distance of the pointer from the middle of the proximity container gets larger as it moves towards the edge, so the animation would slow down instead of speeding up if we were to use this figure as the duration of the animation.

To invert the value stored in the `normalizedDuration` variable, we subtract it from the value representing the middle of the proximity container, and then multiply the resulting figure by 50. The duration argument is in milliseconds, so if we don't use a multiplier (50 was arrived at by trial and error) to increase our value, the animations will occur too quickly.

We can now initiate the animation. We use the JavaScript ternary statement to test whether the `resetOffset` figure is less than 0, and if it is, we know that to get the scroller to slide to the right we just need to set the `left` style property of the scroller element to 0.

If the variable is greater than 0, we have to move the scroller element negatively (to the left) in order to show the images hidden at the right. To align the right edge of the scroller `<div>` element to the right edge of the proximity container, we set the end point of the animation to the `width` of the scroller `<div>` element, minus the `width` of the proximity container.

Time for action – adding the mouse events

Now, we need to add the mouse events that will trigger the animations. The following code will be added below these two lines that we previously added:

```
}, duration, "linear");
}
```

Below the preceding lines, add the following lines of code:

```
prox.mouseenter(function(e) {

  message.text(pointerText).delay(1000).fadeOut("slow");

  goAnim(e);

  prox.mousemove(function(ev) {
    goAnim(ev);
  });
});

prox.mouseleave(function() {
  scroller.stop();
  prox.unbind("mousemove");
});
```

What just happened?

First, we set a mouseeenter event handler so that we can detect when the pointer initially enters the proximity container. When this occurs we change the message text so that it shows what to do with the mouse pointer and then fades out the message slowly after a delay of one second.

We then call our goAnim() function to start the animation. At this point, we set a mousemove event so that we can increase or decrease the speed of the animation as the pointer moves within the proximity container. Each time the pointer moves, we call the goAnim() function once more. Each time this function is called we pass in the event object.

We also set a mouseleave event handler on the proximity container so that we can detect when the pointer leaves this element altogether. When this occurs we stop the currently running animation and unbind the mousemove event handler.

At this point we should have a fully working proximity slider. Earlier, we discussed how the proximity effect is only useful to mouse users, so let's add a keyboard event handler to our script that will let keyboard users navigate the scroller as well.

Time for action – adding keyboard events

Now, we'll be enabling keyboard-driven animations. We'll specifically be adding triggers for the left and right arrow keys on the keyboard.

Add the following code below the prox.mouseleave function that we just added in the preceding section:

```
$(document).keydown(function(e) {

  //37 = left arrow | 39 = right arrow
  if (e.keyCode === 37 || e.keyCode === 39) {

    message.fadeOut("slow");

    if (!scroller.is(":animated")) {
      scroller.stop().animate({
        left: (e.keyCode === 37) ? 0 : -(scroller.width() -
          prox.width())
      }, 6000, "linear");
    }
  }
}).keyup(function() {
  scroller.stop();
});
```

What just happened?

We attach the `keydown` event handler to the `document` object so that the visitor doesn't have to focus the proximity container somehow. Within the anonymous function, we first check whether the left or right arrow keys were pressed.

The key code `37` refers to the left arrow key and the code `39` refers to the right arrow key. The `keyCode` property, normalized by jQuery so that it is accessible to all browsers, will contain the code for whichever key was pressed, but we only want to react to either of the specified keys being pressed.

When either of these keys is pressed, we first fade out the message and then check that the scroller is not already being animated using jQuery's `is()` method in conjunction with the `:animated` filter.

As long as the `scroller` element is not already being animated (denoted by the `!` symbol at the start of the condition), we then animate it. We check the `keyCode` property once again with a JavaScript ternary conditional so that we can move the scroller in the correct direction, depending on which key is pressed.

Finally, we add a `keyup` event handler that stops the scroller animation once the key is released. This improves the interactivity of animation, as it allows the visitor to intuitively stop the scroller whenever they wish.

Have a go hero – extending proximity animations

The obvious way to extend our example would be to trigger animations on the vertical axis as well. We could have a grid of images instead of a single row and animate the grid up and down as well as left and right.

One thing to do to extend the example would be to add additional keyboard functionality. Check for additional keys, such as the home and end keys, for example, which could navigate to the start or end of the `scroller` element accordingly.

Pop quiz – implementing proximity animations

Q1. We provided additional functionality by adding keyboard navigability in the previous example; why?

1. For fun

2. To look good

3. To provide an alternate way for the content to be explored by users that aren't using a mouse

4. Keyboard events must be bound whenever mouse events are used

Q2. Why should we avoid hardcoding 'magic' numbers into our scripts?

1. To make our code more readable

2. So that our scripts are less reliant on the content that they act upon

3. Hardcoded integers take longer to process

4. Because jQuery prefers working with strings

Animating page headers

Another quite fashionable technique is to have an animation that runs in the header of the page when the home page loads. Sometimes the animations run continually on every page of the site; others run once on the home page only.

This technique is an easy and effective way to make your site stand out, and they needn't be complex or heavily apparent animations; a short, subtle animation can be enough to add the WOW! factor.

Earlier in the book, we looked at using **cssHooks** in conjunction with a pre-written file that makes use of cssHooks, which extends jQuery's `css()` method to allow an element's `background-position` style property to be animated. In this example, we'll look at how we can do this manually without the use of the plugin.

Well-written plugins can be an effective and easy solution, but there are times when a plugin adds much more functionality than we actually need, and therefore increases a page's script overhead. It's not often that reinventing the wheel is necessary or advised, but there can be times when it's beneficial to write a custom script that does only what we require.

Time for action – creating an animated header

The underlying page for this example will be relatively straightforward, with just a `<header>` element whose `background-position` we'll animate manually:

1. The header of the example page will consist of just an empty `<header>` element placed inside the `<body>` tag:

```
<header>
</header>
```

2. Save this as `animated-header.html`. The CSS is even simpler, with just a single selector and a few rules:

```
header {
    display:block;
    width:960px;
```

```css
    height:200px;
    margin:auto;
    background:url(../img/header.jpg) repeat 0 0;
}
```

3. Save this as `animated-header.css`. We'll need to link to the file from the `<head>` of the page we just created.

4. The script itself is also surprisingly simple. Add the following code to the function at the end of the `<body>` element:

```javascript
var header = $("header");

header.css("backgroundPosition", "0 0");

var bgscroll = function() {

var current = parseInt(header.css(
    "backgroundPosition").split(" ")[1]),
    newBgPos = "0 " + (current - 1) + "px";

  header.css("backgroundPosition", newBgPos);
};

setInterval(function() { bgscroll() }, 75);
```

5. When we run the file in a browser, we should find that the background image used for the `<header>` slowly scrolls.

What just happened?

In the script we cache the `header` selector outside of our main function for efficiency, so that we aren't creating a new jQuery object every time the function is executed. Even though the `<header>` element is cached in a variable outside of the function, the variable is still accessible by the function.

Within the function we first get the current vertical `background-position` of the `header` element, extracting just the part of the returned string we require using the JavaScript `split()` function. We also use `parseInt` to convert the string into an integer.

We then decrement the integer by one. This means that the background image will scroll up. This is not important. There's no reason why the image couldn't scroll down, I, personally, just happen to prefer motion in the upward direction for some reason. Finally, we set the new `background-position` using jQuery's `css()` method.

After the function definition, we use the JavaScript `setInterval()` method to repeatedly call the function every 75 milliseconds. This is relatively quick, but is quite smooth—much higher than this and the animation begins to get a bit jerky. There's no reason, however, that different background images might not need to run as quickly.

Have a go hero – extending the animated header

As the example is so small, there is a lot that could be done to build on it. Depending on the background image in use, it could be extended to move along the horizontal axis instead, or even both, perhaps moving diagonally in a north-westerly direction.

Animating text using the marquee effect

The use of the `<marquee>` element died out many years ago, but a similar effect, created with JavaScript, is resurfacing in recent years thanks to its use on high-profile sites, such as the tickers for headlines on news sites, and the animated trending topics on the old Twitter home page.

This is an effective and attractive way to present potentially relevant content to the visitor without taking up too much content space. It won't suit all sites, of course, but used sparingly, and in as non-intrusive a way as possible, it can be a great effect.

Time for action – creating and styling the underlying page

In this example, we can see how easy it is to grab a series of text strings and display them in a smoothly scrolling marquee style. We'll use jQuery's built-in AJAX capabilities to grab a JSON file out of the latest posts on my blog. Let's get started.

1. Add the following markup to the `<body>` element of the template file:

```
<div id="outer">
  <header>
    <hgroup>
      <h1>Site Title</h1>
      <h2>Site Description</h2>
    </hgroup>
    <nav>Main site navigation along here</nav>
  </header>
  <article>
    <h1>A Blog Post Title</h1>
    <p>The post copy</p>
  </article>
  <aside>
    <div>
```

```
        <h2>Ads</h2>
          <p>Probably a bunch of ads here that take up a reasonable
            section of this aside vertically</p>
        </div>
        <div>
        <h2>Popular Posts</h2>
          <p>Some links here to other posts, which may or may not
            be related to the current post, but are deemed popular
            based on the number of comments</p>
        </div>
        <div>
        <h2>Related Posts</h2>
          <p>Some links here to other posts that are definitely
            related to this post, based on post tags</p>
        </div>
        <div>
        <h2>Twitter Feed</h2>
          <p>Maybe a twitter feed here that displays recent tweets
            or something. Aside could be quite long by now</p>
        </div>
      </aside>
    </div>
```

2. Save the new page as `marquee.html`.

3. We can also add some basic CSS at this point to layout the example in an acceptable, generic manner. In a new file in your text editor, add the following code:

```css
#outer {
  width:960px;
  margin:auto;
  color:#3c3c3c;
  font:normal 17px "Palatino Linotype", "Book Antiqua",
    Palatino, serif;
}
header {
  display:block;
  padding:0 20px 0;
  margin-bottom:40px;
  border:3px solid #d3d1d1;
  background-color:#e5e5e5;
}
hgroup { float:left; }
h1,
h2 { margin-bottom:10px; }
nav {
```

```
        display:block;
        width:100%;
        height:40px;
        clear:both;
        text-align:right;
    }
    article {
        width:700px;
        height:900px;
        border:3px solid #d3d1d1;
        background-color:#e5e5e5;
        float:left;
    }
    article h1,
    article p { margin:20px; }
    p, nav{
        font:normal 17px "Nimbus Sans L", "Helvetica Neue",
            "Franklin Gothic Medium", Sans-serif;
    }
    p { margin-top:0; }
    aside {
        width:220px;
        height:900px;
        border:3px solid #d3d1d1;
        background-color:#e5e5e5;
        float:right;
    }
    aside div { padding:0 20px 20px; }
```

4. Save this file as `marquee.css` in the `css` directory. Link to this stylesheet from the `<head>` element of the page we just created.

What just happened?

The underlying HTML represents a typical blog. We've added a series of elements for two reasons, primarily so that we have somewhere to insert the marquee, but also so that we can see why this approach can be necessary.

Having the latest posts scrolling across the page near the top of the site ensures that this content is seen straight away, and the fact that it's animated also helps to draw the visitor's attention to it.

The CSS used so far is purely to layout the example elements in a precise and mildly aesthetic way, giving us a generic layout and a light skinning. We'll add some more CSS a little later in the example for our dynamically created marquee. At this point, the page should appear as follows:

Remember, all of the elements in the previous screenshot are there for the marquee to be inserted between. They are not specifically required, and are there for this example.

Time for action – retrieving and processing the post list

Now, we're ready to retrieve the list of latest posts and process them, making them ready to be displayed as items in the marquee. In order to access this data across the Internet from another domain, we need to use **JSONP**, which stands for **JSON with Padding**, and involves dynamically creating and injecting a `<script>` element to the page, although jQuery actually handles this aspect of it for us.

 More about JSONP can be found in these great articles: `http://remysharp.com/2007/10/08/what-is-jsonp` and `http://jquery4u.com/json/jsonp-examples`

1. jQuery provides native support for JSONP and allows us to bypass the same-origin security policy of the browser. In order to output JSON in the correct format, I'm using the JSON API (`http://wordpress.org/plugins/json-api`) plugin on a WordPress-powered blog, which outputs JSON in the following format:

```
{
  "status": "ok",
  "count": 1,
  "count_total": 1,
  "pages": 1,
  "posts": [
    {
      "id": 1,
      etc...
    },
    {
      "id": 2,
      Etc...
    }
  ]
}
```

2. There are more properties in the `posts` array shown in the previous code block, as well as other arrays and properties in the outer object, but the previous snippet should give you an idea of the structure of the data we'll be working with.

3. Add the following code to the anonymous function of our HTML page:

```
$.getJSON("http://adamculpepper.net/blog?json=1&count=10&callba
ck=?", function(data) {

  var marquee = $("<div></div>", {
    id: "marquee"
  }),
  h2 = $("<h2></h2>", {
    text: "Recent Posts:"
  }),
  fadeLeft = $("<div></div>", {
    id: "fadeLeft"
  }),
  fadeRight = $("<div></div>", {
    id: "fadeRight"
  });
  for(var x = 0, y = data.count; x < y; x++) {
```

```
      $("<a></a>", {
        href: data.posts[x].url,
        title: data.posts[x].title,
        html: data.posts[x].title
      }).appendTo(marquee);
    }

  marquee.wrapInner("<div></div>").prepend(h2).append(fadeLeft)
    .append(fadeRight).insertAfter("header").slideDown("slow");

  $("#marquee").find("div").eq(0).width(function() {

    var width = 0;

    $(this).children().each(function() {
      var el = $(this);
      width += el.width() + parseInt(el.css("marginRight"));
    });

    return width;
  });

  marquee.trigger("marquee-ready");
});
```

4. We can also add some more CSS, this time for the newly-created elements. Add the following code to the bottom of `marquee.css`:

```css
#marquee {
  display:none;
  height:58px;
  margin:-20px 0 20px;
  border:3px solid #d3d1d1;
  position:relative;
  overflow:hidden;
  background-color:#e5e5e5;
}
#marquee h2 {
  margin:0;
  position:absolute;
  top:10px;
  left:20px;
}
#marquee a {
```

```
      display:block;
      margin-right:20px;
      float:left;
      font:normal 15px "Nimbus Sans L", "Helvetica Neue",
        "Franklin Gothic Medium", Sans-serif;
    }
    #marquee div {
      margin:20px 0 0 210px;
      overflow:hidden;
    }
    #marquee div:after {
      content:"";
      display:block;
      height:0;
      visibility:hidden;
      clear:both;
    }
    #fadeLeft,
    #fadeRight {
      width:48px;
      height:21px;
      margin:0;
      position:absolute;
      top:17px;
      left:210px;
      background:url(../img/fadeLeft.png) no-repeat;
    }
    #fadeRight {
      left:906px;
      background:url(../img/fadeRight.png) no-repeat;
    }
```

5. When we run the page now, we should see that the new marquee element, along with its links, is inserted into the page.

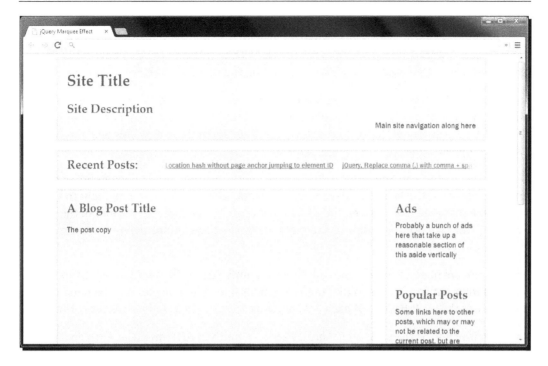

The previous screenshot shows the elements in the new marquee section including the heading, the links themselves, and the fade elements, which are added purely for aesthetics.

What just happened?

All of our JavaScript is wrapped up in jQuery's getJSON() method, which uses jQuery's AJAX functionality to make a request to the URL specified as the first argument to the method. The second argument is an anonymous function that is executed if the request is successful. The returned JSON data is passed to this function automatically.

Within the function we first create some of the elements that make up our marquee including the outer container, the heading, and two purely aesthetic <div> elements used to add the left and right fade effects at the start and end of the row of links. All of these elements are stored in variables so that we can access them easily when required.

Next, we process the JSON object passed into the function. Remember, this object contains a series of properties where the values of some of these properties are arrays, such as the posts array, which contains each of the returned posts as objects within each of its array items.

We use a `for` loop to iterate over each object in the `posts` array that is returned with the JSON object. This object contains a property called `count`, where the number of posts that are returned is stored as an integer, so we can use this to tell the `for` loop how many times to execute, which is marginally easier than counting the objects in the `posts` array.

For each post that has been returned, we create a new `<a>` element, setting its `href` to point to the `url` property of the current object, and the `title` and `text` of the element set to the `title` property of the current object, and then append the new `<a>` element to the `marquee` element that we created a minute ago.

Once we've created and appended a link for each post, we then wrap the contents of the marquee element (the links) in a new `<div>` element, prepend the `<h2>` element to the start of the marquee, and append the `<div>` elements for the fades to the end of the `marquee` element. We then append the marquee to the page before sliding it into view with the `slideDown()` method.

At this point we need to set a `width` on the container's `<div>` element that we wrapped the links in a moment ago. This is so that the links can all line up in a single row. We need to take into account the `width` value of each link, plus any `margin` it has (which we set in the CSS).

We use a function as the value of jQuery's `width()` method to iterate over each link and add its `width` and `margin` to a running total. We can't do this until the marquee has been appended to the page because it is not until this point that each element actually has a `width` or `margin` that we can retrieve.

The last thing we do in the callback function for our `getJSON()` method is fire off a custom event with the `trigger()` jQuery method. The custom event is called `marquee-ready` and is used to tell our script when the `marquee` has been added to the page. We'll use this custom event shortly to animate the post links.

We also added some new CSS to our stylesheet. Some of this code is to give our `marquee` elements the same light skin as the rest of the page. But other parts of it, such as floating the links, and setting the marquee's `overflow` property to `hidden` is so that the links line up in a single row, and so that the majority of the links are hidden, ready to be scrolled into view. We also add the fade images to the last two `<div>` elements inside the `marquee` element.

Time for action – animating the post links

We're now ready to begin scrolling the post links within the marquee. We can do this using our custom event.

1. After the `getJSON()` method, add the following code to the page:

```
$("body").on("marquee-ready", "#marquee", function() {

  var marquee = $(this),
    postLink = marquee.find("a").eq(0);
    width = postLink.width() +
      parseInt(postLink.css("marginRight")),
    time = 15 * width;

  postLink.animate({
    marginLeft: "-=" + width
  }, time, "linear", function() {
    $(this).css({
      marginLeft: 0
    }).appendTo(marquee.find("div").eq(0));
    marquee.trigger("marquee-ready");
  });
});
```

2. Our example is now complete. When we run the page at this point, the posts should begin scrolling from left to right.

What just happened?

We use the jQuery `on()` method to bind an event handler to our custom `marquee-ready` event. We need to use the `on()` event to achieve this, because when this part of the code is executed, the JSON response is unlikely to have returned so the `marquee` element won't even exist. Attaching the event handler to the `<body>` element of the page is an easy way to prepare the page for when the `marquee` element does exist.

Within the anonymous event-handling function, we first cache a reference to the marquee element using the `this` object, which is scoped to our `marquee` element. We then select the first link in the marquee and determine its total `width` including `margin`.

We also work out what is effectively the speed of the animation. jQuery animations use a duration to determine how quickly an animation should run, but the problem this causes us is that posts with longer titles will move faster, because they have a greater distance to animate in the same amount of time.

To fix this, we work out a duration to pass to the animation method based on an arbitrary speed of 15 multiplied by the `width` of the current `<a>` element. This ensures that each post will scroll at the same speed regardless of how long it is.

Once we have obtained the total `width` and `duration`, we can then run the animation on the first link in the `marquee`, using our `width` and `time` variables to configure the animation. We animate the post link by setting a negative `margin` of the first link, which drags all of the other links along with it.

Once the animation is complete, we remove the `margin-left` from the link, re-append it to the end of the `<div>` within the `marquee` element, and fire the `marquee-ready` event once more to repeat the process. This occurs repeatedly, creating the ongoing animation and bringing us to the end of this example.

Have a go hero – extending the marquee scroller

One feature that would certainly be beneficial to our users would be if the post titles stopped being animated when the mouse pointer hovered over them. The animation could then be restarted when the pointer moves off the titles again. Have a go at adding this functionality in, by yourself. It shouldn't be too tricky at all and should involve adding the `mouseenter` and `mouseleave` event handlers.

You'll need to work out how much of any given link is already outside of the visible area of the marquee in order to ensure the animation restarts at the same speed that it stopped at, but this should be quite similar to how we worked out the duration in this version of the example. See how you get on.

Pop quiz – creating a marquee scroller

Q1. Why did we create a dynamic-duration variable (time) instead of using one of jQuery's predefined durations?

1. Because its quicker using an integer, even if that integer has to be calculated, than using one of the duration strings

2. Because it's more fun

3. To make sure the links are appended to the correct element after being animated

4. To ensure that the links all animate at the same speed regardless of how long they are

Summary

In this chapter, the second of our heavily example-based as opposed to theory-based chapters, we looked at some more common animations that are increasingly found on the web. Specifically, we looked at the following types of animations:

◆ A proximity-driven image scroller, where the images scrolled in a certain direction and at a certain speed, depending on the movements of the mouse pointer

◆ Background-position animations, in which we created a continuous-header animation manually with just a few lines of code

◆ A text marquee, where a series of headlines were grabbed from a live Internet feed and displayed in a scrolling marquee-style banner

In the next chapter, we'll move to look at some pure CSS animations that were introduced with CSS3, and how jQuery can be used to enhance them and generally make working with them easier.

9
CSS3 Animations

CSS3 brings many impressive new styles to the web-development arena, and even though the specification is far from complete, many aspects of it are being used in the latest browsers. Pure-CSS animation may even make it into the specification at some point. At the time of writing nearly all modern browsers fully support this. However, with a little help from jQuery we can create our own CSS3 animations that work with varying degrees of success, across all common browsers, new and old.

In this chapter, we'll be covering the following topics:

- The different CSS3 transforms available
- Animating an element's rotation
- Using the CSS3 transforms matrix
- Animating an element's skew with jQuery

 For further information on CSS3 2D transforms, see the W3C Working Draft specification at http://www.w3.org/TR/css3-transforms/.

CSS3 2D transforms

CSS3 defines a style property called `transform` which allows us to transform targeted elements in a two-dimensional space along the x and y axes. A range of transform functions can be supplied as the value of the `transform` property, which dictates how the transformation should be applied. The following 2D transform functions are defined:

Function	Example usage	Description of the transform
matrix	matrix(a, b, c, d, tx, ty)	It rotates, scales, skews, or translates the element according to the combination of the supplied parameters.
rotate	rotate(x)	It rotates the element with a specified number of degree around the transform-origin. By default, the origin should be the center of the element.
scale	scale(x, y)	It scales the element with the specified number of units along the x and y axes. If y is not supplied, it is assumed to be the same as x.
scaleX	scale(x)	It scales the element with the specified number of units along the x axis.
scaleY	scale(y)	It scales the element with the specified number of units along the y axis.
skew	skew(x, y)	It skews the element with the specified number of degree along the x and y axes. If y is not supplied it is assumed to be 0.
skewX	skew(x)	It skews the element with the specified number of degree along the x axis.
skewY	skew(y)	It skews the element with the specified number of degree along the y axis.
translate	translate(x, y)	It repositions the element with the specified number of pixels along the x and y axes. If y is not provided it is assumed to be 0.
translateX	translate(x)	It repositions the element with the specified number of pixels along the x axis.
translateY	translate(y)	It repositions the element with the specified number of pixels along the y axis.

Understanding the matrix

All the individual transform functions (`rotate()`, `skew()`, among others) can be thought of as shortcuts for a specific matrix transform. Indeed, most browsers will apply a matrix behind-the-scenes even when a transform function is provided.

The `matrix` function takes six parameters, and each of the transforms mentioned in the previous table can be performed by providing different combinations of values for these parameters. Sometimes we can apply several transforms simultaneously by using the `matrix` function. Let's look at some quick examples to illustrate how the matrix can be used.

Translate

Translating an element causes it to move from its original location. Positive values translate the element to the right or down the page (depending on the axis), and negative values move the element to the left or up the page. For example, an element could be moved 100 pixels right along the x axis and 100 pixels down along the y axis using the following transformation matrix:

```
transform: matrix(1, 0, 0, 1, 100, 100);
```

This `matrix` function, equivalent to using the transform function `translate(100px, 100px)`, would cause the targeted element to appear like the following screenshot:

As we can see in the previous screenshot, the element has moved from its original location (upper-left corner of the screen) even though we have not used CSS to position the element, which we can see is the case in the DOM Inspector.

The fifth parameter of the matrix in this example corresponds to the x axis, and the sixth parameter to the y axis. Don't worry too much about the first four parameters as we will cover these in more detail shortly.

 It is of critical importance to note that some browsers, such as Firefox, expect these values with the units specified (as in the previous screenshot), while other browsers, such as Opera, or those based on the WebKit rendering engine, will expect these values without units.

An element does not need to be positioned in order for it to be translated, and the transform does not affect the flow of the document or other elements around it. Adjacent elements will position themselves according to an element's original location, not its new location following a translation. The translated element's content is also translated along with it.

Scale

You may be wondering why we supplied the value 1 as the first and fourth parameters in our first matrix code snippet, but 0 as the value of the second and third parameters instead of supplying all zeros.

The reason for this is that, the parameters (the first and fourth) correspond to the `scale` transform function, so to retain the transformed element's original size, the `scale` parameters are set to 1. To double the size of an element (without translating its position), we could use the following transformation matrix:

```
transform: matrix(2, 0, 0, 2, 0, 0);
```

This snippet would be equivalent to using `transform: scale(2, 2)` and would cause the targeted element to appear like this:

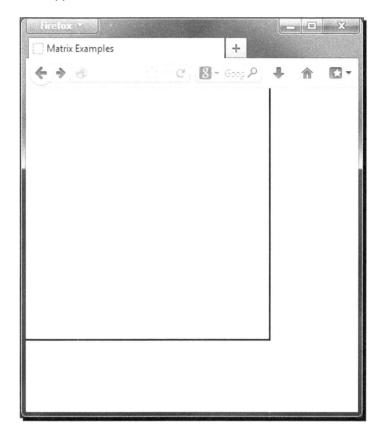

In the previous screenshot we can see that the element is now twice its original size.

The previous code symmetrically scales the target element along both the x and y axes. These values are unitless in all supporting browsers, and the value 0 cannot be specified. Integers or floating-point numbers may be provided, and the scaling may be asymmetrical if necessary.

An interesting effect of scaling is that, providing negative values cause the element to be reversed, and not shrunk, as we may intuitively surmise. So if we were to provide -2 and -2 as the first and fourth values in the previous code snippet, the element would be reflected both vertically and horizontally, as well as being made twice its original size. We can even supply a combination of positive and negative values for this type of transformation.

A reflected element would appear like this:

The element is reversed along both its x and y axis, as if it were being viewed upside down in a mirror. This could be hugely useful if, for example, we were implementing pure-CSS reflections.

Skew

The two zero values that correspond to the second and the third parameters in the matrix can be used as skew values, with the x axis using the second parameter, and the y axis using the third. We could skew an element (without modifying its scale or position) using the following matrix transform function:

```
transform: matrix(1, 1, 0, 1, 0, 0);
```

The following screenshot shows a skewed element:

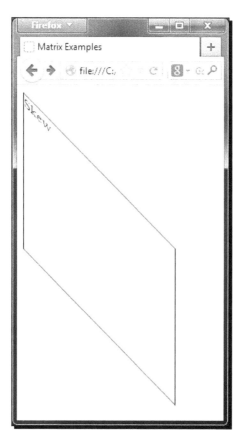

The previous screenshot shows an element skewed along the x axis. As with other matrix functions, positive values for these parameters cause transformation along the right or downwards direction, negative values along the left or upward direction.

In the previous snippet, only the x axis has been skewed. A consequence of the skew is that the element has grown in size. The bounding box of the transformed element has doubled in size from 200 px (the original size of the element) to 400 px.

Regardless of this increase in size however, the flow of the document remains unaffected by the transform and just like the other transforms, any content within the transformed element also becomes transformed.

 Transforms have a varying impact on any text contained in the element across different browsers, with the text remaining crisp and readable in some browsers following a transform, and degrading in other browsers.

Rotation

To rotate an element using the matrix, we need to use the trigonometric functions sine and cosine to calculate the values of the first four parameters. The first and the fourth parameters take cosine functions of the angle of rotation, while the second and the third parameters are sine and minus-sine functions of the rotation respectively.

 The sine and cosine functions are relatively advanced mathematical constructs used to express the different relationships between the sides of triangles and the angles of triangles.

While an understanding of their exact nature is not essential to use them (JavaScript has built-in functions that will calculate them automatically), a deeper understanding of their nature and use will only help when working specifically with rotation.

For a basic introduction, see the Wikipedia article on Trigonometric functions at `http://en.wikipedia.org/wiki/Trigonometric_functions`.

To rotate an element by, for example, 37 degrees we would use the following transform:

```
transform: matrix(0.7986355, 0.6018150, -0.6018150, 0.7986355, 0, 0);
```

Our rotated element should appear like this:

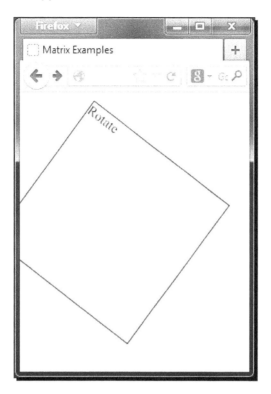

As we can see, the edges of the rotated element appear outside of the viewport. Care should be taken to correctly position elements that are to be rotated so as to ensure that there is adequate space to display the element in its entirety if necessary.

Calculating the sine and cosine functions of the angle of rotation can be easily done using a scientific calculator, or of course JavaScript itself programmatically.

Working with transforms

Using the shortcut transform functions such as `rotate()` or `skew()` is easier and more convenient than using the matrix. However, this ease of use comes at a price—we're limited to using only one of them at a time on a single element. If we were to try and use more than one of them in a CSS statement, only the last one defined would be applied.

If we need to apply several different transforms to an element, we can use the matrix function, depending on which transformations we need to apply. For example, we can skew an element, while also translating and scaling it using something like the following:

```
transform: matrix(2, -1, 0, 2, 300px, 0);
```

In this example, the element would be skewed along the x axis, doubled in size, and moved 300 px to the right. We couldn't rotate the targeted element in the previous code snippet at the same time as doing these things.

Even if we supply two matrix functions, one for the skew, scale, and translate, and a second for the rotation, then only the rotation would be applied. We can however rotate and translate, or rotate and scale an element simultaneously using a single matrix function.

Using jQuery and transforms

We can use jQuery's `css()` method in the setter mode to set the CSS3 transforms on selected elements, and we can use it in getter mode to retrieve any transform functions set on an element. We just need to ensure that we use the correct vendor prefix, such as `-moz-transform` for Firefox, or `-webkit-transform` for WebKit/Blink-based browsers. Opera also has its own vendor prefix (for older versions), as do newer versions of IE.

One thing to be aware of is that while we can set a specific transform function such as `rotate()` on a selected element, we can only get the value of the `style` property in its matrix format. Have a look at the following code:

```
$("#get").css("-moz-transform", "rotate(30deg)");
$("#get").text($("#get").css("-moz-transform"));
```

This would result in the following:

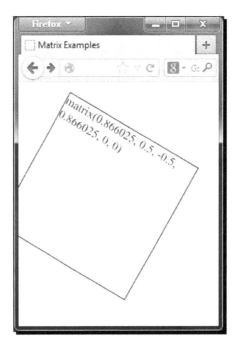

In the previous screenshot, we see that the rotation we applied in the first line of code using the `rotate()` transform function is returned with the second line of code as a matrix function.

cssHooks

It's important to note that the use of `cssHooks` could help with browser compatibility testing on your code for all the various vendor prefixes. More about `cssHooks` can be found here: `http://api.jquery.com/jQuery.cssHooks/`.

Also, a great jQuery plugin for `cssHooks` can be found here: `https://github.com/brandonaaron/jquery-cssHooks`. It has some CSS3 2D transforms behavior included. While it is beneficial from a learning perspective to create these effects manually, as we do throughout the remainder of this chapter, remember to use this file to save your time and effort in the future.

CSS3 3D transforms

All of the transform functions we have looked at so far are two-dimensional, operating on just the x and y axes. Transforms that operate in three dimensions, along the x, y, and z axes have also been proposed.

3D equivalents of all of the transform functions exist and usually just take an extra parameter, which corresponds to the vector of each dimension, and the angle. For example, a 3D rotation could be added using this code:

```
transform: rotate3d(0, 1, 0, 30deg);
```

As with 2D transforms, there is an all-encompassing matrix function that allows us to implement any of the other transforms and allows us to combine some of them together on a single element.

If, like me, you thought the 2D transform matrix, with its six parameters, was complex and perhaps a little hard to understand, wait till you start using the 3D matrix, which has 16 parameters in total!

At present, 3D transforms are supported in WebKit-based browsers and Firefox (with partial support for IE10), so we won't be looking at these in any further detail.

Browser support for CSS3 3D transforms can be found here: `http://caniuse.com/transforms3d`.

Animated rotation with jQuery and CSS3

In this example, we'll set up an animation that rotates an image using the `rotate()` transform function. Since this is supported by the majority of common browsers, it's actually really easy to implement, and can be a great effect that enhances the appearance and behavior of the page it is used on.

Time for action – animating an element's rotation

We'll just be rotating a simple image in this example, so this is the only visible element we need in the `<body>` element of the page.

1. Add the following `<img>` tag to a fresh copy of the template file:

```
<img src="img/color-wheel.png" id="colorWheel">
```

At this point we don't even need any styles as everything we need to set can be done in the JavaScript which we'll add next.

2. In the anonymous function at the bottom of the HTML page, add the following code:

```
var img = $("#colorWheel"),
  offset = img.offset(),
  origWidth = img.width(),
  origHeight = img.height(),
  rotateStrings = [
    "rotate(",
    0,
    "deg)"
  ],

  getVendor = function() {

  var prefix = null,
    vendorStrings = {
    pure: "transform",
    moz: "-moz-transform",
    webkit: "-webkit-transform",
    op: "-o-transform"
  };

  for (props in vendorStrings) {
    if (img.css(vendorStrings[props]) === "none") {
      prefix = vendorStrings[props];
    }
  }
```

```
    if (prefix === null) {
      prefix = "filter";

      img.css({
        position: "absolute",
        filter: "progid:DXImageTransform.Microsoft.Matrix(
          sizingMethod='auto expand');"
      });
    }

    return prefix;
  },
vendor = getVendor();

function doRotate() {

  rotateStrings[1]++;

  if (vendor === "filter") {
    var rad = rotateStrings[1] * (Math.PI * 2 / 360),
      cos = Math.cos(rad),
      sin = Math.sin(rad),
      driftX = (img.width() - origWidth) / 2,
      driftY = (img.height() - origHeight) / 2,
      el = img.get(0);

    img.css({
      left: offset.left - driftX,
      top: offset.top - driftY
    });
      el.filters.item("DXImageTransform.Microsoft.Matrix")
        .M11 = cos;
      el.filters.item("DXImageTransform.Microsoft.Matrix")
        .M12 = -sin;
      el.filters.item("DXImageTransform.Microsoft.Matrix")
        .M21 = sin;
      el.filters.item("DXImageTransform.Microsoft.Matrix")
        .M22 = cos;

  } else {
    img.css(vendor, rotateStrings.join(""));
  }
}

setInterval(function() { doRotate() }, 100);
```

3. Save the page as `rotate.html`. If we run the page in a browser now, we should see the color wheel slowly spinning around its center.

What just happened?

The first thing we did was to cache a selector for the image as we'll be referring to it several times throughout the code. Note that, this is the only jQuery object we created in the whole script, which as we've discussed earlier in the book, is great for improving performance.

We also set some other variables at this point including the offset of the image (its `absolute` position on the page), its original width and height, and an array containing different parts of the CSS property that we'll set in string and integer formats.

We also set an inline function (`getVendor()`) as the value of a variable which we can use to determine which vendor prefix to use. This function first sets some variables which will be used to store the determined vendor prefix and an object literal containing all of the different prefixes we want to test for. We also include the native `transform` property. Although this isn't yet supported by any browser, one day it might be, so this helps future-proof our code.

The `doRotate()` function iterates over each property in the object literal using a `for...in` loop. Within the loop, we try to read the value of the `transform` property using each vendor prefix. An interesting fact is that, each browser will report `none` as the value of the prefix it supports, and a falsey value such as `false`, `null`, or `undefined` for the prefixes it doesn't support. We can use this to reliably determine which browser is in use and therefore which vendor prefix we need to use. The correct vendor prefix for whichever browser is in use is then saved to the `vendor` variable ready to be returned.

 If none of these tests identify a vendor prefix, then it's likely that the browser in use is an older version of Internet Explorer. Again, keep in mind, jQuery 2.0 does not support IE8 and below.

If the vendor variable is still set to null at this point, we set the variable to `filter`. In order to programmatically work with the value of the `filter` property in IE, `filter` must already be applied to the element, so we also set a filter on the element in this part of the code using jQuery's `css()` method ready to manipulate later in the code. We also set the `sizing mode` to `auto expand` in order to prevent the element from being clipped when the rotate is applied.

At the end of the function the `prefix` variable is returned containing a string of the vendor prefix for the browser currently in use. Directly after the function, we set a variable called `vendor` which will contain the value returned by the function for easy reference.

Next, we define a regular function `doRotate()` which will be used to perform the actual rotation. The first thing we do in this function is increment the second property of our `rotateStrings` array by one.

We then check whether the `vendor` variable equals `filter`. If it does, we know that the browser in use is IE and can proceed to determine the values that the proprietary `filter` will need. IE allows rotation to be implemented in two different ways. We could use the `BasicImage` filter property to rotate the image, although that allows us only to set one of four rotation values: `0`, `1`, `2` or `3`, which correspond to 0, 90, 180, or 270 degrees. This is simply not flexible enough for our needs in this example.

So, instead we use the `Matrix` filter which gives us much more control over the degree of rotation. This is very similar to the CSS3 matrix transform, with six parameter values that are combined to generate the different transforms (a rotation in this case).

The parameters that we use in this example are `M11`, `M12`, `M21`, and `M22` which map roughly to the first four values in the CSS3 version, with the exception that the second and the third values are reversed in Microsoft's vendor prefix version.

The values of each of these properties must be computed using the JavaScript trigonometry functions, `Math.cos` and `Math.sin`. We set some variables to calculate these values. The first variable, `rad`, converts the number of degrees of rotation into radians as these are the units required by the `Matrix` filter. The radians are calculated by multiplying the current degree of rotation (stored as the second item in our `rotateStrings` array) by PI times 2, divided by 360.

An unfortunate problem that occurs in IE when rotating elements is that, the rotated element drifts around the page as it is being rotated. This is caused by the size of the element's bounding box increasing as the element rotates. The rotation does occur around the center of the element, but because IE thinks the element has grown, the center of the rotated element is shifted on each rotation.

The `drifX` and `driftY` variables that we set, allow us to determine how far the element has shifted so that we can correct it. The shift is worked out by comparing the original width and height of the element prior to it being rotated, with the new width and height following the rotation.

We also store the raw `img` element from the jQuery object using jQuery's `get()` method with an argument of `0` which returns the actual DOM node instead of a jQuery object. The `filter` must be applied to a proper DOM element.

Once we've set our variables, we then correct the drift caused by the previous rotation using jQuery's `css()` method, and then insert our computed trigonometry values into the `Matrix` filter.

Finally, if the `vendor` variable equals anything other than `filter`, we can simply set the relevant vendor prefix to the items in our `rotateStrings` array. We do this by calling JavaScript's `join()` method on the array. This is much more efficient than using concatenation to create the string needed for the CSS property and as this function will be executed repeatedly, we really need to make sure it is as efficient as possible.

The last thing we do in our code is start the rotation animation by setting an interval that calls our `doRotate()` function every 100 milliseconds. We use an anonymous function as the first argument of the `setInterval()` function which avoids the need to attach the function to be executed be saved to the `window` object.

Problems with IE

Besides the fact that IE makes us work twice as hard as any other browser to set the element's rotation, it also presents us with another problem: it totally destroys the alpha layer of the PNG we are rotating. Suddenly our nice anti-aliased circle-edge becomes jagged and unsightly (view this example in IE to see the issue).

The animation is also slightly jerky in IE, and both this and the inability to use PNGs with alpha layers in them could easily be a show-stopper for IE. If this was the case, we could easily disable the animation in IE by simply doing nothing when the `filter` property is returned by our `getVendor()` function. There are some things we could do however, to negate the problems in IE.

For example, we could simply use a PNG with no transparency, which would preserve the circle's border in IE (in this example). Or, we could lay another image over the top of the image we are rotating to hide the jagged edges.

Pop quiz – implementing CSS3 rotation

Q1. In this example we used an array in conjunction with the JavaScript `join()` method to create the string. Why?

1. Because it's more fun.

2. Because it makes our code look better.

3. Because performance-wise, it's much faster than string concatenation.

4. Because otherwise the element won't rotate correctly.

Q2. To make the animation run correctly in Internet Explorer we had to constantly adjust the `top` and `left` style properties of the rotated element in order to maintain its position. Why does the drift in IE occur?

1. Because the size of the rotated element's bounding box is changed throughout the animation. As the rotated element is centered within its bounding box, its position changes as the box increases and decreases in size.

2. Because the alpha layer of the PNG was removed.

3. Because the Matrix filter property was used.

4. Because of a bug in IE's implementation of the CSS3 rotate property.

Have a go hero – extending CSS3 rotation

The rotation effect can be used in many places, whether animated or not. But when animated, as in this example, it makes a very good background as part of a larger composition of elements. Used as the background of a semi-transparent logo for example, it creates a stunning effect.

Have a go at incorporating the effect into a page and using it as the background of another image. You'll also see first-hand how much this can improve the appearance of the effect in IE.

Animated skewing

Just like with the `rotate()` function, we can animate a `skew()` transform for creating attractive special effects. In this example, we'll use the `matrix()` function for all browsers, not just IE, in order to apply several transforms to an element at once.

The context of this example will be a cover-flow style widget that displays images one after the other by animating the images' skew. The user will be able to cycle back and forth through the images using links:

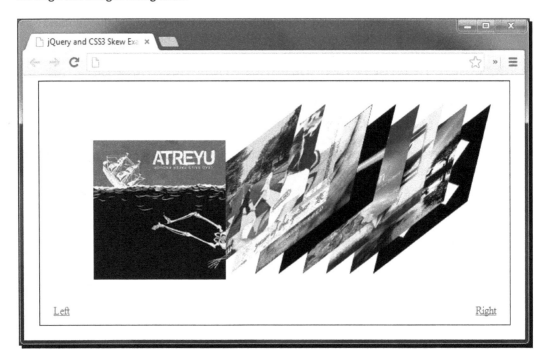

The previous screenshot shows how the finished widget will appear.

Time for action – creating the underlying markup and basic styling

First, we'll look at the HTML that we'll be using in the example and then we'll look at the initial styling added to the elements prior to being skewed.

1. Add the following code to the `<body>` element of the template file:

```
<div id="viewer">
  <div id="flow">
    <img src="img/atreyu.jpg">
    <img src="img/beatles.jpg">
    <img src="img/blink.jpg">
    <img src="img/cold.jpg">
    <img src="img/disturbed.jpg">
    <img src="img/floyd.jpg">
    <img src="img/korn.jpg">
```

```
      <img src="img/prodigy.jpg">
      <img src="img/the-birthday-massacre.jpg">
      <img src="img/xx.jpg">
   </div>
   <ul>
      <li id="left"><a href="#" title="Move Left">Left</a></li>
      <li id="right"><a href="#" title="Move Right">
         Right</a></li>
   </ul>
</div>
```

2. Save the page as `skew.html`. Next, in a new file add the following code:

```
#viewer {
  width:700px;
  height:220px;
  padding:100px 0 30px;
  margin:auto;
  border:1px solid #000;
  position:relative;
}
#flow:after {
  content:"";
  display:block;
  height:0;
  clear:both;
  visibility:hidden;
}
#flow img {
  display:block;
  margin-left:-165px;
  position:relative;
  top:-15px;
  left:245px;
  float:left;
  background-color:#fff;
}
#viewer li {
  list-style-type:none;
  position:absolute;
  bottom:10px;
}
#left { left:20px; }
#right { right:20px; }
```

3. Save this file in the `css` directory as `skew.css`.

What just happened?

We're using a simple collection of elements for this example. We used an outer container, mostly for positioning purposes so that we can center the widget in the viewport and position other elements within it.

The <img> elements are what we will be applying the skew animations to, so these are isolated in their own container to make selecting them in the script later on easier. We also have a list element containing two links. These will be used to trigger the animations.

The CSS is as light as the HTML. We simply position the container, the images, and the controls as required for the example. All of the fun CSS3 we'll set and manipulate using the script. You should note that this example isn't progressively enhanced as this would deviate too far from an already quite large example, as we'll see in a moment when we add the JavaScript.

Time for action – initializing the widget

The first thing we need to do is set up the images ready to have their skew manipulated. We can also add the function that will return the correct vendor-specific prefix for the transform style property that we used in the last example. In the empty function at the bottom of the HTML page, add the following code:

```
var viewer = $("#viewer"),
  flow = viewer.find("#flow"),
  order = flow.children().length,
  oneRad = 1 * (Math.PI / 180),
  matrix = ["matrix(", 1, ",", 0, ",", 0, ",", 1, ",",
    "0px,", "0px)"],
  msMatrix = "progid:DXImageTransform.Microsoft.Matrix(
    sizingMethod='auto expand')",
  getVendor = function() {
    var prefix = null,
      vendorStrings = {
        pure: "transform",
        moz: "-moz-transform",
        webkit: "-webkit-transform",
        op: "-o-transform"
      };

    for (props in vendorStrings) {
      if(flow.css(vendorStrings[props]) === "none") {
        prefix = vendorStrings[props];
      }
    }
```

```
    if (prefix === null) {
      prefix = "filter";
    }

    return prefix;
  },
  vendor = getVendor(),
  property = (vendor !== "filter") ? matrix.join("") : msMatrix;

flow.children().eq(0).addClass("flat").css(vendor,
  property).css("zIndex", order + 1);

flow.children().not(":first").each(function(i) {

  el = flow.children().eq(i + 1);

  matrix[1] = 0.7;
  matrix[3] = -30 * oneRad;
  matrix[5] = -10 * oneRad;
  matrix[7] = 0.7;
  matrix[9] = (vendor === "-moz-transform") ? "90px," : "90,";
  matrix[10] = (vendor === "-moz-transform") ? "-30px)" : "-30)";

  if (vendor !== "filter") {
    el.addClass("skew-right").css(vendor,
      matrix.join("")).css("zIndex", order);
  } else {
    el.addClass("skew-right").css(vendor, msMatrix).css({
      zIndex: order,
      top: -30,
      left: 270,
      width: 140,
      height: 140,
      marginLeft: -100
    });
    el.get(0).filters.item("DXImageTransform.Microsoft.Matrix")
      .M11 = 1;
    el.get(0).filters.item("DXImageTransform.Microsoft.Matrix")
      .M12 = matrix[5];
    el.get(0).filters.item("DXImageTransform.Microsoft.Matrix")
      .M21 = matrix[3];
    el.get(0).filters.item("DXImageTransform.Microsoft.Matrix")
      .M22 = 1;
  }
```

```
    order--;

});

matrix[3] = 0;
matrix[5] = 0;
```

What just happened?

In the first part of the script we initialize our variables. If you've wondered why we always initialize our variables at the top of functions, the reason is because of a phenomenon called Hoisting. This is where the variables initialized in functions get "hoisted" to the top of the function and can contain results that we aren't expecting.

 You can learn more about JavaScript Hoisting at: http://thecomputersarewinning.com/post/a-dangerous-example-of-javascript-hoisting/.

The first variable we create is a cached selector for the outer container of our widget. This is the one and only jQuery object we create in this entire example. Some of the code we'll add is quite intensive in places, so keeping the number of jQuery objects we create to a bare minimum is essential for performance reasons.

Next we use the original jQuery object and the find() jQuery method to cache a selector for the flow element (the direct parent of the image elements that will be skewed) as we'll need to access or manipulate this element several times as well.

Then we store the number of image elements in the widget using the length property of a jQuery object containing the child elements of the flow element. We also store the result of converting one degree to one radian so that we can easily convert from one unit to another throughout the script without repeatedly performing the same calculation. Both the CSS3 transform matrix and IE's matrix filter can accept radians so that makes them a convenient unit to work with.

We then create our matrix array and Microsoft's matrix property as a string. The array includes all of the individual properties as array items, including the required commas as strings. The reason we include the commas in our array is that we can call the join() JavaScript function on the array later without specifying a separator and without having to worry about removing the unnecessary commas it would insert incorrectly.

Next we add the `getVendor()` function that we used in the previous example. This is a convenient way to ensure that correct prefix is used when we apply the skew styling. We won't cover this function in detail as we have already looked at it earlier in the chapter (in the *Time for action – animating an element's rotation* section). Again, we call the function straight away after defining it and store the result in a variable for later use.

The last variable we create will hold a string containing either the CSS3 matrix function with all the required parameters, or it will contain IE's `matrix` property in its most basic form with only the `sizingMethod` parameter defined. If you remember from the previous example, IE can only manipulate the matrix property after it has been initially set.

At this point we can move on to prepare the first image. We select the first image using jQuery's `eq()` method, passing in 0 as the index of the element we are interested in. We set a class name of `flat` on the first image so that we can easily select it later, and also give it a higher `z-index` than the other images so that it is visible in its entirety. Next we loop through the remaining images using jQuery's `each()` method.

The anonymous function we pass to the method accepts the parameter `i` which is the index of the current iteration. This in turn will allow us to select each element one after the other on each iteration of the loop. The first thing we do in the function is cache a reference to the current `<img>` element using the index as an argument for the `eq()` method. We add 1 to the index value to avoid selecting the first image.

In the next block of code we set some of the items in our `matrix` array. We set the scale parameters (items 1 and 7 in the array) to 0.7 so that the skewed images are reduced in size slightly and we set the skew parameters (items 3 and 5 in the array) to the radian equivalent of -30 and -10 degrees respectively. This will skew the images slightly up and to the right.

We also set the translate parameters (items 9 and 10 in the array) to position the skewed elements correctly so that they stack up horizontally. If the browser in use is Firefox we have to use `px` in the value for the translate properties, but with other browsers the values should be unitless. We use a ternary condition to check the `vendor` variable (this will contain the vendor prefix for the current browser) and set the value accordingly.

Once we've set our array items we then check whether the browser in use is not IE and provided it isn't, we apply the skew to the current element. We also set the `z-index` of the current element using the `order` variable which is set to the length of the number of images. Doing this makes the current element the top-most image.

If the browser in use is IE, we apply the Microsoft `matrix` and set some different CSS on the images. The translate parameters don't work in IE, so we position the images using jQuery instead. Skewing the elements in IE also causes the elements to increase in size, so we have to drastically reduce their dimensions which we also do with jQuery.

On each iteration of the loop we reduce the value of this variable by one. The z-index of each element will therefore get progressively lower as we process each image.

Once we have set the required CSS styles, we then skew the elements by manipulating the proprietary Microsoft `matrix` filters. Remember, these properties can only be manipulated on actual DOM elements, not jQuery objects, so we retrieve the raw element using jQuery's `get()` method with the index as 0.

After the `each()` loop has finished, we reset the third and fifth parameters in the `matrix` array. This is because we will use the array again several times, so each time we should use the default values for the parameters.

Time for action – animating an element's skew

Now we'll add a function that will skew the elements to the left. The function will have to be applied to two elements: to the flat or non-skewed element, as well as to the one before it (to the right in this case). The function to animate the skew from right to left is as follows and should be placed below the `matrix[5] = 0;` line:

```
function skewRTL() {

  var flat = flow.find(".flat").css("zIndex", order + 1),
    preFlat = flat.next(),
    flatMatrix = matrix.slice(0),
    preMatrix = matrix.slice(0),
    flatDims = 200,
    preDims = 170,

  skew = function() {

    if (preFlat.length) {

      if (flatMatrix[3] <= 30 * oneRad && flatMatrix[5] <=
        10 * oneRad) {

        var flatTranslateX = parseInt(
          flatMatrix[9].split("p")[0], 10),
          flatTranslateY = parseInt(
            flatMatrix[10].split("p")[0], 10),
          preTranslateX = parseInt(
            preMatrix[9].split("p")[0], 10),
          preTranslateY = parseInt(
            preMatrix[10].split("p")[0], 10);
```

```
flatMatrix[1] = flatMatrix[1] - 0.001;
flatMatrix[3] = flatMatrix[3] + oneRad;
flatMatrix[5] = flatMatrix[5] + (oneRad / 3);
flatMatrix[7] = flatMatrix[7] - 0.001;
preMatrix[1] = preMatrix[1] + 0.01;
preMatrix[3] = preMatrix[3] + oneRad;
preMatrix[5] = preMatrix[5] + (oneRad / 3);
preMatrix[7] = preMatrix[7] + 0.01;
flatMatrix[9] = (vendor === "-moz-transform") ?
  flatTranslateX - 6 + "px," : flatTranslateX - 6 + ",";
preMatrix[9] = (vendor === "-moz-transform") ?
  preTranslateX - 3 + "px," : preTranslateX - 3 + ",";
preMatrix[10] = (vendor === "-moz-transform") ?
  preTranslateY + 1 + "px)" : preTranslateY + 1 + ")";

if (vendor !== "filter") {
  flat.css(vendor, flatMatrix.join(""));
  preFlat.css(vendor, preMatrix.join(""));
} else {
flat.get(0).filters.item(
  "DXImageTransform.Microsoft.Matrix")
  .M12 = flatMatrix[5];
flat.get(0).filters.item(
  "DXImageTransform.Microsoft.Matrix")
  .M21 = flatMatrix[3];
preFlat.get(0).filters.item(
  "DXImageTransform.Microsoft.Matrix")
  .M12 = preMatrix[5];
preFlat.get(0).filters.item(
  "DXImageTransform.Microsoft.Matrix")
  .M21 = preMatrix[3];
  flatDims = flatDims - 2;
  preDims = preDims + 0.5;

  flat.css({
    width: flatDims,
    height: flatDims
  });
  preFlat.css({
    width: preDims,
    height: preDims
  });
}

} else {
```

```
        clearInterval(flatInterval);

        if (vendor !== "filter") {
          preMatrix[3] = 0;
          preMatrix[5] = 0;
          preFlat.css(vendor, preMatrix.join(""));
        } else {
          flat.css({
          top: -30,
          left: 260
        });
        }

        flat.prev().css("zIndex", "");
        flat.removeClass("flat").css("zIndex", "");
        preFlat.addClass("flat");
      }
    } else {

      clearInterval(flatInterval);
      flat.css("zIndex", order + 1);
    }
  };

  preMatrix[3] = -30 * oneRad;
  preMatrix[5] = -10 * oneRad;

  if(!flatInterval) {
    var flatInterval = setInterval(function() { skew() }, 1);
  }
};
```

What just happened?

The first thing we did in our function is we set the variables used by the function. We cached a reference to the current element that has the `flat` class and also set this element's `z-index` to be one higher than any of the other images to ensure it is always on top of the other images.

We also cached a reference to the next image after the `flat` image. In this function, this will be the image to the right of the un-skewed image. We then made two copies of the original `matrix` array, one for the `flat` element and one for the `preFlat` element. To copy an array, all we did is use JavaScript's `slice()` method with an index of zero.

The next two variables we created are the initial dimensions of the `flat` and `preFlat` images. These variables are only used by IE, but because of hoisting, we need to define them here and not in an IE-specific code block later in the function.

Next we defined an inline function called `skew()` which we'll repeatedly call in order to produce the actual animation. Within this function we first checked that there is an element after the `flat` element by checking that the `preFlat` object has a length. If the length is equal to zero (that is if it does not have length), we simply clear any intervals that may exist, and make sure that the `flat` element is at the top of the z-index stack. If the `preFlat` object does have a length however, we then check that the current `skewX` property is less than or equal to the radian equivalent of 30 degrees, and that the `skewY` property is less than or equal to the radian equivalent of 10 degrees (we can work this out by multiplying 30 or 10 respectively by our stored figure for 1 radian). The current skew properties for the `flat` image are currently stored in items the third and fifth items in the `flatMatrix` array.

Provided both conditions are true, we can proceed with the animation. Part of the animation involves translating the `flat` and `preFlat` images so that along with skewing, the images move as well (we'll also resize them, but we'll come to that in a moment).

In order to translate the images correctly we need to get their current translation, which we do first of all by defining four new variables and populating them with the current translation values from the two matrix arrays. These figures need to be numerical so we use JavaScript's `parseInt` and `split()` functions to break the strings apart and convert the digits to integers.

Next we needed to update our two matrix arrays with the new values. The right-to-left function will incrementally update the values in the `flatMatrix` and `preMatrix` arrays, and then apply the arrays to the element. So the animation will consist of rapid updates to each transform parameter.

The `flat` image also needs to be skewed as it is translated, so we increase the `skewX` and `skewY` parameters by one radian and a third of one radian respectively. Remember, in order to skew an element to the left and up directions, the skew parameters should be positive so we increase the values of items 3 and 5 of the `flatMatrix` array on each pass of the function.

The `flat` image starts off larger than the skewed images so we need to reduce array items 1 and 7 slightly, each time the function runs. The `skew()` function will be called 30 times; so to reduce the scale of the flat image so that it finishes the correct size, we reduce the scale parameters by `0.001` on each pass of the function.

The values we want are 30 degrees of the skew on the x axis, and 10 degrees of the skew on the y axis. 10 is one third of 30 which is why we increase the `skewY` parameter by one radian divided by three.

I mentioned earlier that in Firefox the translate parameters need a unit, such as `px`, but other browsers are unitless for these values. We use a JavaScript ternary conditional to check the `vendor` string and if it equals the Firefox vendor prefix (`-moz-transform`), we add `px` to the value. The flat image only needs to be translated on the x axis and it needs to move left by 6 pixels, so we update array item 9 with a value that is six less than its current value.

We also have to update the `preFlat` image so that it goes from being skewed to the right to being flat. We also have to increase the size of the `preFlat` image as they start out smaller. Similarly, we updated the relevant array items in the `preMatrix` so that over the course of 30 iterations of the `skew()` function they end up at the right values. The `preFlat` image also needs to be translated, but this time along both the x and y axes.

Next we checked the vendor string once more and as long as it isn't `filter` (IE), we apply the transform to the `flat` and `preFlat` image by joining the array. If it is IE, we have to do a little more work to apply the transformation.

We applied each of the relevant `Matrix` properties, `M12` and `M21`, on the `flat` and `preFlat` images. We used jQuery's `get()` method with an index of `0` to obtain the actual DOM element once more. We also reduced the size of the `flat` image, and increased the size of the `preFlat` image using our `flatDims` and `preDims` variables that we initialized earlier and then we used jQuery's `css()` method to apply the new sizes.

IE's `Matrix` property helpfully ignores the scaling parameters when the `sizingMethod` is set to `auto expand`, but this property must be set to prevent the images from being clipped. This is why we fallback to jQuery's `css()` method.

Unusually, we were able to set fractional pixel sizes when using IE, which is fortunate as it allows us to set the size of the images in the correct order for them to end up at the right size when the animation ends.

We then come to the last part of the `skewRTL()` function before we start our animation. This block of code is executed once at the end of the animation when the third and fifth items in our `flatMatrix` array are greater than 30 and 10 respectively.

First we cleared the intervals so that the skew is not animated further. We then check the vendor string once more, and as long as it isn't `filter`, we reset the skew on the flat element to `0` (on both the x and y axes).

This is needed because for some reason, the `preFlat` image doesn't quite go back to exact zero. I assume this is because JavaScript's `Math` functions do not allow the number to have enough decimal places to be entirely accurate. The image is only slightly off however, so this sudden switch to `0` at the end of the animation is not noticeable.

Unfortunately, translating an element at the same time as skewing it does not seem possible in IE. What happens is that IE applies the new skew, but fails to apply the new position until the skew animation has finished, so the element is skewed and then moved in two separate steps. It doesn't look too great, so instead, after the skew animation is complete, we simply reposition the flat element without animating it.

After correcting the skew or the position, we remove the z-index from the flat element (which has now been skewed to the left) and remove the class name flat from it, and then add the class name flat to the preFlat element.

At this point the flat image has been skewed to the left, resized and translated, and the preFlat image has been skewed back to zero, resized and translated. Both the flat and preFlat images are transformed together at the same time, which is why the function is as large as it is.

Right at the end of the skewRTL() function, defined after the skew() function that will be repeatedly called by the setInterval() function, we initialize the third and fifth values in the preMatrix array so that the array will contain the correct skew for the initial state of the element. When we create the array by copying the original matrix array used when the widget is initialized, these items will both be set to 0.

Before calling the setInterval() function on the two images to be skewed, we first check that an interval doesn't already exist. This stops the widget from breaking if the link is repeatedly clicked by the visitor. The element will be skewed more than once if the link is clicked several times in rapid succession, but the widget will continue to function and the page will not throw errors.

Time for action – skewing an element from left to right

We can now add the function that skews an element from left to flat and from flat to right. This function is very similar to the function we just looked at. The changes in the code have been highlighted in the following code:

```
function skewLTR() {

    var flat = flow.find(".flat"),
        preFlat = flat.prev(),
        flatMatrix = matrix.slice(0),
        preMatrix = matrix.slice(0),
        flatDims = 200,
        preDims = 170,

        skew = function() {
```

```
if (preFlat.length) {

  if (flatMatrix[3] >= -30 * oneRad && flatMatrix[5] >=
    -10 * oneRad) {

    var preTranslateX = parseInt(preMatrix[9].
      split("p")[0], 10),
    preTranslateY = parseInt(preMatrix[10].
      split("p")[0], 10);
    flatMatrix[1] = flatMatrix[1] - 0.001;
    flatMatrix[3] = flatMatrix[3] - oneRad;
    flatMatrix[5] = flatMatrix[5] - (oneRad / 3);
    flatMatrix[7] = flatMatrix[7] - 0.001;
    preMatrix[1] = preMatrix[1] + 0.01;
    preMatrix[3] = preMatrix[3] - oneRad;
    preMatrix[5] = preMatrix[5] - (oneRad / 3);
    preMatrix[7] = preMatrix[7] + 0.01;
    preMatrix[9] = (vendor === "-moz-transform") ?
      preTranslateX + 3 + "px," : preTranslateX + 3 + ",";
    preMatrix[10] = (vendor === "-moz-transform") ?
      preTranslateY + 1 + "px)" : preTranslateY + 1 + ")";
    if (vendor !== "filter") {
      flat.css(vendor, flatMatrix.join(""));
      preFlat.css(vendor, preMatrix.join(""));
    } else {
      flat.get(0).filters.item(
        "DXImageTransform.Microsoft.Matrix")
        .M12 = flatMatrix[5];
      flat.get(0).filters.item(
        "DXImageTransform.Microsoft.Matrix")
        .M21 = flatMatrix[3];
      preFlat.get(0).filters.item(
        "DXImageTransform.Microsoft.Matrix")
        .M12 = preMatrix[5];
      preFlat.get(0).filters.item(
        "DXImageTransform.Microsoft.Matrix")
        .M21 = preMatrix[3];

      flatDims = flatDims - 1.5;
      preDims = preDims + 1.5;

      flat.css({
        width: flatDims,
        height: flatDims
      });
```

```
            preFlat.css({
              width: preDims,
              height: preDims
            });
          }

      } else {

          clearInterval(flatInterval);
          clearInterval(preInterval);

          if (vendor !== "filter") {
            preMatrix[3] = 0;
            preMatrix[5] = 0;
            preFlat.css(vendor, preMatrix.join(""));
          }

          flat.removeClass("flat").css("zIndex",
            parseInt(flat.next().css("zIndex")) + 1);
          preFlat.addClass("flat").css("zIndex", order + 1);


        }
    } else {
      clearInterval(flatInterval);
      clearInterval(preInterval);
      flat.css("zIndex", order + 1);
    }
  };

  order = flow.children().length;
  preMatrix[3] = 30 * oneRad;
  preMatrix[5] = 10 * oneRad;
  preMatrix[9] = (vendor === "-moz-transform") ? "-90px," : "-90,";
  preMatrix[10] = (vendor === "-moz-transform") ? "-30px," :
    "-30,";

  if(!flatInterval) {
    var flatInterval = setInterval(function() { skew() }, 1),
    preInterval = setInterval(function() { skew() }, 1);
  }
};
```

What just happened?

We won't cover the whole function in its entirety as it's very similar to what we have discussed before, but let's take a moment to look at what differs in this function. First, instead of selecting the next image to the right of the `flat` element, we select the one to the left of it using jQuery's `prev()` method instead of `next()`.

When updating the skew on our `flat` and `preFlat` elements, we are skewing the element the opposite way. To skew an element to the right, we need to use a minus figure so instead of going from 0 to 30 or from -30 to 0, we are going the opposite way, from 30 to 0 or 0 to -30, so we subtract the radian equivalent of 1 degree instead of adding it.

We are also translating to the right instead of the left, so instead of removing 3 pixels each time to move the image left we add 3 pixels to move it to the right. We also provide different values for the dimensions variables used by IE.

This time when we set the `z-index` of the element that was previously flat, we add 1 to the z-index of the next element (to the right) to make sure it is higher than this element. However, we can't use our length variable (`order`) from earlier or it will be at the same `z-index` as the `flat` element, but will appear above it as it comes after the element in the DOM.

The final difference is that when we initialize the third and fifth items in our array, we are specifying the current skew to the left and not the right, so these items are set to the radian equivalent of 30 and 10 degrees instead of -30 and -10.

Time for action – wiring up the controls

All that's left to do is add the event handlers to the left and right links at the bottom of the widget so that the different images can be viewed. After the two skew functions, add the following code:

```
viewer.find("#left a").click(function(e) {
  e.preventDefault();
  skewRTL();
});

viewer.find("#right a").click(function(e) {
  e.preventDefault();
  skewLTR();
});
```

What just happened?

All we do is add a click handler to each link which prevents the link from being followed with `preventDefault` and then call the relevant skew function. The example should now be fully working in all common browsers, although the effect is handled rather badly by IE in general with slower, more sluggish animations, less accurate skewing, jittery, and uncontrollable movements.

One point to note is that there is a difference between the full and minified versions of the jQuery source file which causes older versions of IE to throw errors when the minified version is used, but not when the un-minified version is used.

Have a go hero – extending matrix animation

It would definitely be beneficial to build this example so that it incorporates progressive enhancement. Work on an alternative, accessible layout that works with the scripting disabled, and then convert the widget into the format used in this example.

You could also work on a more suitable fallback for IE, in which the example uses a simpler image viewer, perhaps one of those looked at earlier in the book.

Pop quiz – using the matrix

Q1. The CSS3 matrix transform function is useful in which situation?

1. When we want to work in radians instead of degrees.
2. When we need to animate a transform function.
3. When we want to apply more than one transform function to an element.
4. When coding for Internet Explorer.

Q2. In the transform function `matrix(a, b, c, d, e, f)`, which parameters refer to the element's translation?

1. a and b
2. a and d
3. b and c
4. e and f

Summary

In this chapter we looked at CSS3 transform style properties in detail, covering some of the different transform functions, including:

- `matrix`
- `rotate`
- `scale`
- `scaleX`
- `scaleY`
- `skew`
- `skewX`
- `skewY`
- `translate`
- `translateX`
- `translateY`

We learned a lot about the CSS3 `matrix` property in this chapter, as well as how to make use of it with jQuery. Specifically, we learned the following:

We first saw the different values that these functions take and the effects that they have on elements they are applied to. We also saw that in order to animate these styles, we can use simple native JavaScript intervals or timeouts to continuously adjust the function parameters, or apply them in a rapid sequence. We learned that, in most cases these transform functions can only be applied to elements individually, we also saw that only the last transform function that is defined is applied to the elements. The matrix function however allows us to apply several of the functions to a single element.

We learned that we can't rotate and skew a single element, but we can rotate, scale, and translate an element, or skew, scale, and translate it if we wish. Browser support for CSS3 transforms is very good, with only very minor differences between most browsers.

We observed that although we can't use the transform functions in jQuery's `animate()` method, we can easily create our own animations manually, and we can use them with other methods, such as the `css()` method. Don't forget to use `cssHooks` (see the previous tip) to achieve this kind of functionality too.

In the next and final chapter of the book, we'll take a look at a new HTML5 element that allows us pixel-perfect control over an area on the page—the `<canvas>` element—and how it can be used to create interactive animations.

10

Canvas Animations

In the last chapter, we looked at one of the latest CSS3 features, the `transform` property, which enabled us to create animated rotations, skews, scales, and translates. In this chapter, we're going to look at one of the new additions to HTML5—the `<canvas>` element.

The best way to think of the `<canvas>` element is to treat it like the kind of canvas on which an artist would paint. We can draw simple lines or complex shapes using JavaScript API methods, and there is also support for images and text. The canvas is two-dimensional at this point, but may be extended to include 3D support in the future.

The `<canvas>` element, first proposed and used by Apple, has been implemented by most modern browsers, and is considered one of the most stable elements from the HTML5 specification.

The best description of the `<canvas>` element I've seen states, "A canvas is a rectangle in your page where you can use JavaScript to draw anything you want, from `diveintohtml5.info`", which sums it up quite nicely I feel.

Subjects that we'll look at in this chapter will include:

- ◆ The HTMLCanvasElement interface
- ◆ Drawing to the `<canvas>` element
- ◆ Animating the `<canvas>` element
- ◆ Using `<canvas>` with jQuery
- ◆ Creating a `<canvas>` based game

Learning the HTMLCanvasElement interface

The HTMLCanvasElement interface exposes methods and properties allowing us to define and control the shapes that are drawn on the canvas. The HTMLCanvasElement interface can be broken down into distinct sections depending on what the methods do.

Using the canvas element

The `<canvas>` element itself has methods that can be called on it, including:

Method	Usage
`getContext(a)`	Returns an object (a `CanvasRenderingContext2D` object to be precise) which can then have other methods from the API called on it to manipulate the `<canvas>` element. The argument specifies the type of context to retrieve. Only two-dimensional contexts are available at present.
`toDataURL()`	Returns a data URL representing the image on the `<canvas>` element. Optional arguments include the type of image represented by the data URL (with the default being image/PNG), and any arguments specific to the type, such as the quality for image/JPG data URLs.

The `<canvas>` element can be thought of as being similar to an `<img>` element that doesn't have a `src` attribute. Allowed attributes include the `width` and `height` parameters of the element, along with an `id` and a `class` attributes, among others. There are no special attributes associated with the `<canvas>` element, although it can contain other elements. When the browser cannot display the `<canvas>` element, it can display the element's content as a fallback. The only properties of the `<canvas>` element we have access to, are the `width` and `height` parameters. Setting either of these properties causes the `<canvas>` element to reset its contents to nothing, which can be useful when we want to clear it.

Understanding context methods

There are two methods that relate directly to the context object returned by the `getContext()` method. These are:

Method	Usage
`save()`	Saves the current state of the canvas; only transforms are saved, not shapes or paths.
`restore()`	Restores the saved state.

We can also set a couple of global properties that apply to all shapes on the `<canvas>` element. These properties are:

Property	Usage
`globalAlpha`	Sets the alpha transparency of shapes. Takes a decimal value between 0.0 and 1.0.
`globalCompositeOperation`	Sets how shapes stack up on top of one another. Can be used to create masks and clear areas of shapes.

Native shapes

The `<canvas>` element has just one native shape defined: the rectangle. One important point to note here is that the `<canvas>` element does not have an internal DOM tree—shapes or paths we draw on the `<canvas>` element are not created as child elements of the `<canvas>` element and cannot be accessed with standard DOM manipulation methods. They are not individual objects, they are just pixels. Methods from the scripting API used specifically when working with rectangles include the following:

Method	Usage
`clearRect(a, b, c, d)`	Removes all shapes and paths from an area of the canvas. Arguments a and b specify the coordinates to begin clearing at and arguments c and d specify the width and height of the area to clear.
`fillRect(a, b, c, d)`	Draws a rectangle. Arguments a and b specify the coordinates to begin drawing at and arguments c and d specify the width and height of its sides.
`strokeRect(a, b, c, d)`	Draws the outline of a rectangle. Arguments a and b represent the starting coordinates of the shape, and arguments c and d represent the width and height of its sides.

We can set the color of strokes (outlines) or fills, as well as drop-shadows using the following properties:

Property	Usage
`fillStyle`	Sets the color of the fill. Can be set to a CSS color or a gradient object.
`shadowBlur`	Sets the amount of blur on the shadow.
`shadowColor`	Sets the color of the shadow. Can be set to a CSS color or a gradient object.
`shadowOffsetX`	Sets the relative position of the shadow along the x axis.
`shadowOffsetY`	Sets the relative position of the shadow along the y axis.
`strokeStyle`	Sets the color of the stroke. Can be set to a CSS color or a gradient object.

These properties can be set on paths and text as well. They aren't limited strictly to the native shape.

Drawing using a path

Any shape other than a rectangle must be drawn using a path. This gives us a flexible way of drawing custom and complex shapes. Some of the methods used for creating paths include:

Method	Usage
`arc(a, b, c, d, e, f)`	Draws a circular subpath. Arguments a and b are the starting coordinates of the subpath, c is the radius, d is the starting angle in radians, and e is the ending angle in radians. The last parameter f accepts a Boolean indicating whether the subpath should be drawn anticlockwise or not.
`arcTo(a, b, c, d, e)`	Draws a circular subpath to a specified point. Arguments a and b are the starting coordinates, c and d are the ending coordinates. Argument e is the radius.
`beginPath()`	Starts a new path.
`bezierCurveTo(a, b, c, d, e, f)`	Draws a subpath along a Bezier curve, which is a curve featuring two control points. Arguments a, b, c, and d represent the coordinates of the two control points and arguments e and f represent the end coordinates of the subpath.
`closePath()`	Closes the path by drawing a line from the current position to the starting position of the first subpath in the current path list.
`fill()`	Colors the shape created by the current path.
`lineTo(a, b)`	Creates a new subpath from the current location to the coordinates specified as arguments.
`moveTo(a, b)`	Moves to the coordinates specified by the arguments without drawing a new subpath.
`quadraticCurveTo(a, b, c, d)`	Draws a subpath along a quadratic curve, which is a curve with a single control point. Arguments a and b represent the coordinates of the control point, while arguments c and d represent the end coordinates of the subpath.
`stroke()`	Colors the outline of the current path list.

Paths have several properties that can be set including the style, the line, or cap, or how paths are joined:

Property	Usage
lineCap	Can be set to either butt (the default), round, or square.
lineJoin	Can be set to either miter (the default), round, or bevel.
lineWidth	A decimal specifying the width of the path.
miterLimit	Determines the length between the inner point where two paths connect and the outer point before the join is mitered.

Drawing images and patterns

The canvas allows us to draw images to the canvas in the same way that we might assign a background image to another element. We can also draw patterns based on images or gradients. This category of methods includes:

Method	Usage
drawImage(a, b, c)	Draws an image on the <canvas> element. Argument a is the image to be drawn and arguments b and c are the coordinates to place the top-left point of the image. Note that other variants of this method exist which allow different combinations of arguments allowing images to be scaled and sliced.
createPattern(a, b)	Draws a repeated pattern on the <canvas> element. Argument a is the image to be used as the pattern and b is the type of repeat.
createLinearGradient(a, b, c, d)	Creates a linear gradient between two points. Arguments a and b are the start coordinates of the gradient and c and d are the end coordinates.
createRadialGradient(a, b, c, d, e, f)	Creates a radial gradient between two circles. Arguments a and b are the start coordinates, and c is the radius of the first circle. Arguments d and e are the start coordinates of the second circle, and f is its radius.
addColorStop(a, b)	Adds color to a gradient. The first argument is a decimal between 0.0 and 1.0 and is the relative position within the gradient to add the color. The second argument is the color to use.

The `drawImage()` and `createPattern()` methods are very similar; in that they are both used to draw an image on the `<canvas>` element. The difference is that the pattern is repeated. The gradient methods return a gradient object which can then be used as the fill or stroke style for a shape.

Text strings

Text strings can be written to the canvas, but there is little styling we can perform on them as there is no associated box model with the text; so that means, no padding, margins, or borders. However, we can set the font and alignment, along with the fill color or stroke color using other properties. These methods include:

Method	Usage
`fillText(a, b, c)`	Creates solid text strings on the `<canvas>` element. The first argument, a, is the text to write and arguments b and c are the start coordinates of the text.
`measureText(a)`	Measures the specified text string and returns a metrics object with a width property.
`stroketext(a, b, c)`	Creates outline text strings on the `<canvas>` element. The first argument is the text to write and arguments b and c are the start coordinates of the text.

The properties we can set on text include:

Property	Usage
`font`	Sets the size and the font-family of the text.
`textAlign`	Sets the alignment of the text. Can be either `start` (the default), `end`, `left`, `right`, or `center`.
`textBaseline`	Sets the baseline of the text. Can be either `alphabetic` (the default), `top`, `hanging`, `middle`, `ideographic`, or `bottom`.

Applying transformation methods

The `<canvas>` element can have the same transforms applied to it that we saw in the last chapter, which can be applied using the following methods:

Method	Usage
rotate(a)	Rotates a shape by the specified number of radians.
scale(a, b)	Scales a shape along each axis by the specified amount, with a being the x axis and b the y axis.
translate(a, b)	Translates the shape along each axis by the specified amount, with a being the x axis and b the y axis.
transform(a, b, c, d, e, f)	The transform() method is equivalent to the matrix transform form function and can be used in the same way to scale, translate, and/or skew the shape.
setTransform(a, b, c, d, e, f)	Resets the current transform to the identify matrix, and then invokes the transform() method using the same arguments. This essentially undoes the current transformation, and then sets the specified transform, all in one step.

Pixel manipulation

The <canvas> element even allows us to work directly with the pixels in the canvas and can retrieve shapes as imageData objects, or create shapes directly by manipulating the <canvas> element at pixel-level. We have the following methods for manipulating pixels:

Method	Usage
createImageData(a, b)	Creates a new, blank imageData object using the supplied arguments as width and height properties. This method can also be passed to another imageData object, which will cause the method to return an (empty) imageData object the same width and height as the original.
getImageData(a, b, c, d)	Returns an imageData object containing the pixel data for the specified area of the <canvas> element. Arguments a and b are the start coordinates of the area, and arguments c and d are the width and height.
putImageData(a, b, c)	Paints the pixel data to the <canvas> element. The first argument is the imageData object to use, the second and third are the start coordinates of the resulting shape.

All `imageData` objects, either those we get from the `<canvas>` element, or those we create with the `createImageDate()` method have several properties we can make use of, including:

Property	Usage
data	This property is a `CanvasPixelArray`, and is read-only when we get an `imageData` object from the `<canvas>` element. We can also use it to set the pixel data in an `imageData` object we create. The array contains four items per-pixel: the `r`, `g`, and `b` values for the pixel, and the alpha.
height	The height of the image is represented by the `imageData` object. This property is read-only.
width	The width of the image is represented by the `imageData` object. This property is read-only.

Drawing to the canvas

Drawing to the `<canvas>` element programmatically is very straightforward in theory. The methods and properties are easy to use, and are quite consistent between supporting browsers. Direct pixel manipulation is the trickiest part of the API to master, but other than that there is nothing really complicated.

One thing we do find is that our code can very quickly mount up. As soon as we're drawing multiple complex shapes, and setting various properties, our code can easily run to a few hundred lines or more even for relatively simple drawings. This is especially true when animating the contents of the `<canvas>` element.

Time for action – drawing to the canvas

Let's take a look at a quick example of drawing a non-animated shape. We don't even need jQuery for this.

1. Add the `<canvas>` element to the `<body>` tag of our template file:

```
<canvas id="c" width="500" height="300">
  <p>Your browser doesn't support the canvas element!</p>
</canvas>
```

2. Next we can add the JavaScript that will draw to the `<canvas>` elements. We'll draw a Union Jack flag. Function in the `<script>` element at the bottom of the template file and add the following code in its place:

```
var canvas = document.getElementById("c"),
  context = canvas.getContext("2d");
```

```
context.fillStyle = "#039";
context.fillRect(50, 50, 400, 200);

context.beginPath();
context.strokeStyle = "#fff";
context.lineWidth = 50;
context.moveTo(250, 50);
context.lineTo(250, 250);
context.moveTo(50, 150);
context.lineTo(450, 150);
context.moveTo(50, 50);
context.lineTo(450, 250);
context.moveTo(50, 250);
context.lineTo(450, 50);
context.stroke();
context.closePath();

context.strokeStyle = "#C00";
context.lineWidth = 30;
context.beginPath();
context.moveTo(250, 50);
context.lineTo(250, 250);
context.moveTo(50, 150);
context.lineTo(450, 150);
context.stroke();
context.closePath();

context.lineWidth = 1;
context.fillStyle = "#C00";

context.beginPath();
context.moveTo(50, 50);
context.lineTo(195, 125);
context.lineTo(165, 125);
context.lineTo(50, 66);
context.fill();
context.closePath();
context.beginPath();
context.moveTo(450, 50);
context.lineTo(305, 125);
context.lineTo(275, 125);
context.lineTo(422, 50);
context.lineTo(450, 50);
context.fill();
```

```
context.closePath();

context.beginPath();
context.moveTo(450, 250);
context.lineTo(310, 175);
context.lineTo(335, 175);
context.lineTo(450, 235);
context.lineTo(450, 250);
context.fill();
context.closePath();

context.beginPath();
context.moveTo(50, 250);
context.lineTo(200, 175);
context.lineTo(225, 175);
context.lineTo(80, 250);
context.lineTo(50, 250);
context.fill();
context.closePath();
```

3. Save the file as `canvas.html`.

4. If we run the page now in any modern browser, we should see something like the following screenshot:

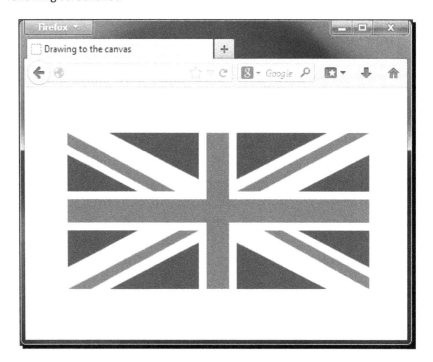

5. In the previous screenshot, we can see the simple arrangement of geometric shapes that make up the British flag (note that the flag is not completely to the scale). Images like this are easy to produce using the `<canvas>` element but even simple shapes can require a lot of code.

What just happened?

The first thing we do is get the `<canvas>` element using the JavaScript's `getElementById()` method, and then get the two-dimensional context object from the `<canvas>` element with the `getContext()` method. We can now interact with the `<canvas>` element via the context object.

We set some of the color for the context using the `fillStyle` property, and then draw a solid rectangle using the `fillRect()` method. The arguments specified are the starting x and y locations of the rectangle, and the width and height.

The filled rectangle picks up the fill style that we have just set, which is deep blue, and will form the background of the flag. We now need to create a white horizontal and diagonal cross on top of the blue background. We can do this by drawing two thick lines across the middle of the flag, one vertical and one horizontal. We'll use paths for this, so we start a new path using the `beginPath()` method.

Next, we set the color of the stroke to white using the `strokeStyle` property, and the width of the path using the `lineWidth` property. To draw a path we have to tell the `<canvas>` element (or the context object actually) where to start the path, which we do using the `moveTo()` method, specifying the coordinates to move to as arguments (the top middle of the rectangle).

To make the path, we then use the `lineTo()` method and specify the coordinates of where to end the path (the bottom-middle of the rectangle). This gives us the vertical line. To make the horizontal path, we repeat the same process, moving to the left-middle of the rectangle and drawing to the right-middle.

Coordinates specified using the `moveTo()` method are always relative to the canvas itself with `0, 0` representing the top-left corner of the canvas. This is the same for the `lineTo()` method as well, even though the line that is drawn begins at the point specified by the last call of `moveTo()`.

Next, we need to make a diagonal white cross over the background rectangle and the vertical cross, which we'll do by drawing paths in the same way as before using the combinations of `moveTo()` and `lineTo()` methods.

All of the paths we've added so far are part of the same path—they are subpaths, and at this point, they aren't actually visible. To make them visible, we need to either fill or stroke them, so we stroke them with the `stroke()` method and then close the path with the `closePath()` method.

For the next part of the flag, we need to draw a slightly thinner red cross over the white cross. We'll use another path for this. We set the new color style and width, and draw a new path across the center of the rectangle vertically and horizontally again.

To complete the flag, we need to add four more shapes to make the diagonal parts of the red cross. We can't use straight-line paths for these because they don't intersect, and they are all positioned slightly differently. This means that we have to draw them manually as custom shapes and fill them.

These four shapes actually make up the majority of the code, but we're basically doing very similar things as before. Each shape is made by drawing subpaths and filling them. We use a new path for each shape to preserve the anti-aliasing of the lines. If we used one big path for all four shapes, the edges of the shapes would be jagged.

Pop quiz – drawing to the canvas

Q1. What arguments are required for the `fillRect()` method?

1. The x and y location of the rectangle
2. The width and height of the rectangle
3. The x and y location of the rectangle, its width and height, and its color
4. The x and y location of the rectangle, and its width and height

Q2. What method is required to make a path visible?

1. `strokeStyle` and `lineWidth`
2. `moveTo()` and `lineTo()`
3. `stroke()` or `fill()`
4. `closePath()`

Have a go hero – creating the flag of your nation

If you're not from the UK, have a go at drawing the flag of your own nation on the canvas. We can create compositions of repeated shapes using standard JavaScript for loops, so use this to your advantage in keeping the code required for your flag as minimal as possible. If you are from the UK, try recreating a favorite logo or icon.

If part of your flag (or logo) is extremely complex, remember that we can draw images to the <canvas> element as well as lines and shapes, so feel free to draw out the basic part of your flag using the <canvas> element drawing methods, and then use an image for the complex part.

Animating the canvas

The <canvas> methods we've looked at so far are easy to use and nothing, if not a little, repetitive. Animating the objects on the <canvas> element is where things start to get interesting. Animating is harder than simply drawing on the <canvas> and as we have no real way of debugging it other than trial and error, solving bugs can quickly become problematic and somewhat time-consuming.

In our flag example, there was no real benefit to using the <canvas> element. We could have got exactly the same effect, with much less code and processing, by simply including an image of the flag on our page. However, animating the <canvas> element is where its benefits really begin. This is where we can do much more than anything we could achieve with a simple image. The additional complexity that animating the <canvas> element entails is totally worth it.

Time for action – creating an animation on the canvas

In this example, we'll draw the same flag as we did before, except that this time we'll animate different shapes. The underlying HTML used in this example is exactly the same as in the previous examples. All that changes is the content of the <script> element at the end of the <body> element.

1. To make the working file for this example, just remove everything in the <script> element at the bottom of canvas-explorer.html and resave the file as canvas-animated.html.

2. The first thing we'll do is bring the blue rectangle in from the side of the canvas to the center of the <canvas> element. Add the following code to the now empty <script> element at the bottom of the page:

```
(function() {

  var canvas = document.getElementById("c"),

  init = function(context) {

    var width = 0,
      pos = 0,
      rectMotion = function() {
```

```
            if (width < 400) {
              width = width + 2;
              context.fillStyle = "#039";
              context.fillRect(0, 50, width, 200);
            } else if (pos < 50) {
              pos = pos + 2;
              canvas.width = 500;
              context.fillStyle = "#039";
              context.fillRect(pos, 50, 400, 200);
            } else {
              clearInterval(rectInt);
              whiteLines(context);
            }
          },
          rectInt = setInterval(function() { rectMotion() }, 1);
      };
      if (window.ActiveXObject) {
        window.onload = function() {
          var context = canvas.getContext("2d");
            init(context);
        }
      } else {
        var context = canvas.getContext("2d");
        init(context);
      }
    })();
```

What just happened?

In the previous examples in this chapter all of our variables were global, which is generally bad practice when coding for the real world. In this example, our code is within the scope of the anonymous function, so the variables are only accessible within that function and are therefore not considered global.

Within the init() function, we declare the width and pos variables and then define another inline function called rectMotion(), which will be called repeatedly by an interval. Any shapes drawn outside of the bounds of the <canvas> element do not exist, so we can't draw a rectangle out of view and then animate it into view. Instead, we gradually build up the rectangle by starting at the left edge and incrementally widening the rectangle until it is the correct width.

This is done using the first branch of the if statement, which will be executed while the width variable is less than 400. To speed the animation up, we actually increase the width of the rectangle by two pixels at a time (although the speed of the animation is also considerably different between browsers) by increasing the width variable and then using the variable as the width argument in the fillRect() method.

Once the width variable has reached 400, we then change over to use the pos variable instead. In this part of the condition, we increase the pos variable by two (the rectangle will appear to move two pixels at a time, again for speed), reset the <canvas> element by setting its width, and set the fillStyle property. We then draw the new rectangle, using the pos variable as the argument for the x axis position.

It will look as if the rectangle is being moved to the right, but this is not the case at all. We are actually destroying the rectangle and then drawing a completely new one that's two pixels to the right of the original.

Once the rectangle is in the correct location, we clear the interval and then call the next function, (we'll add this shortly) passing in the context object. After the rectMotion() function, we add a final variable that contains the ID of the interval which calls the function to animate the rectangle. We use this variable to clear the interval once the animation is complete.

If you run the page in a browser at this point, the blue rectangle appears to move into the <canvas> element from the left before stopping in the middle. Next, we need to animate the horizontal and diagonal white crosses over the blue rectangle.

Time for action – animating the white crosses

In this part of the animation, we'll draw a white line down the middle and across the center of the rectangle, and then make the diagonal cross grow out from the center to the corners. The following code should be added in between the canvas and init variables in the code so far:

```
whiteLines = function(context) {

  context.fillStyle = "#fff";
  context.strokeStyle = "#fff";
  context.lineWidth = 50;

  var width = 0,
    height = 0,
    pos = {
      ne: { x: 250, y: 150 },
      se: { x: 250, y: 150 },
```

```
        nw: { x: 250, y: 150 },
        sw: { x: 250, y: 150 }
      },
    growDiagonal = function() {
      if (pos.ne.x >= 50) {
      context.beginPath();
      context.moveTo(pos.ne.x, pos.ne.y);
      context.lineTo(pos.ne.x - 4, pos.ne.y - 2);
      context.moveTo(pos.se.x, pos.se.y);
      context.lineTo(pos.se.x - 4, pos.se.y + 2);
      context.moveTo(pos.nw.x, pos.nw.y);
      context.lineTo(pos.nw.x + 4, pos.nw.y + 2);
      context.moveTo(pos.sw.x, pos.sw.y);
      context.lineTo(pos.sw.x + 4, pos.sw.y - 2);
      context.stroke();
      context.closePath();

      pos.ne.x = pos.ne.x - 2;
      pos.ne.y = pos.ne.y - 1;
      pos.se.x = pos.se.x - 2;
      pos.se.y = pos.se.y + 1;
      pos.nw.x = pos.nw.x + 2;
      pos.nw.y = pos.nw.y + 1;
      pos.sw.x = pos.sw.x + 2;
      pos.sw.y = pos.sw.y - 1;
      } else {
      clearInterval(crossInt);
      redCross(context);
      }
    },
  growVertical = function() {

    if (height < 200 || width < 400) {
      if (height < 200) {
        height = height + 2;
        context.fillRect(225, 50, 50, height);
      }
      if (width < 400) {
        width = width + 4;
        context.fillRect(50, 125, width, 50);
      }
    } else {
      clearInterval(rectInt);
      crossInt = setInterval(function() { growDiagonal() }, 1);
    }
  },
  rectInt = setInterval(function() { growVertical() }, 1);
},
```

What just happened?

Essentially we have another inline function, which contains another function that gets repeatedly called with another interval. As we're drawing white crosses this time, we need to set some style properties (we'll be drawing both lines and rectangles in this function and so set the `fillStyle` and `strokeStyle`) as well as the `lineWidth` property.

We initialize the `width` and `height` control variables, which will be used to control how many times the interval runs, and we also store the starting positions of the vertical and diagonal crosses in an object called `pos`.

We then define two inline functions, one to create the vertical cross and the other to create the diagonal cross. The `growVertical()` function is called first with an interval and we just draw one white rectangle from top to bottom, and one from left to right in the center of the background using the `width` and `height` variables to repeat the interval as many times as necessary. The interval is cleared once the rectangles are of the correct size and then the `growDiagonal()` function is called with another interval.

In this function we need to draw four lines, each starting in the middle of the vertical cross. We use the different properties in our `pos` object to do this. Each time the function is executed, we move to the x and y positions specified for each line in the object and then draw towards the relevant corner. We then update the properties in the object ready for the next iteration of the function.

Each property needs to be updated by different amounts, for example, the line moving from the center to the top-left of the rectangle needs to move negatively along both the x and y axes, whereas the line to move to the top-right corner needs to move positively along the x axis, but negatively along the y axis. We use a new path on each iteration of the function to preserve the anti-aliasing of the lines.

Once the lines are drawn, we clear the interval and call the next function. We'll define this function now. It should be placed after the `canvas` variable, but directly before the `whiteLines()` function that we just added.

Time for action – animating the red crosses

All we need to do now is draw the vertical red cross and the four custom red shapes. Add the following code in between the `rectInt` variable declaration near the top of the `<script>` element and the `whiteLines` function we defined in the previous section:

```
redCross = function(context) {
  context.fillStyle = "#C00";
  context.strokeStyle = "#C00";
  context.lineWidth = 30;
```

```
var width = 0,
  height = 0,
  pos = {
    up : { x: 250, y: 150 },
    down : { x: 250, y: 150 },
    left: { x: 250, y: 150 },
    right: { x: 250, y: 150 }
  },

  addStripes = function() {
    context.lineWidth = 1;

    function makeStripe(props) {
      context.beginPath();
      context.moveTo(props.startX, props.startY);
      context.lineTo(props.line1X, props.line1Y);
      context.lineTo(props.line2X, props.line2Y);
      context.lineTo(props.line3X, props.line3Y);
      context.fill();
      context.closePath();
    }

    setTimeout(function() { makeStripe({
      startX: 50, startY: 50,
      line1X: 195, line1Y: 125,
      line2X: 165, line2Y: 125,
      line3X: 50, line3Y: 66
    })}, 1);
    setTimeout(function() { makeStripe({
      startX: 450, startY: 50,
      line1X: 305, line1Y: 125,
      line2X: 275, line2Y: 125,
      line3X: 422, line3Y: 50
    })}, 50);
    setTimeout(function() { makeStripe({
      startX: 450, startY: 250,
      line1X: 310, line1Y: 175,
      line2X: 335, line2Y: 175,
      line3X: 450, line3Y: 235
    })}, 100);
    setTimeout(function() { makeStripe({
      startX: 50, startY: 250,
      line1X: 200, line1Y: 175,
```

```
            line2X: 225, line2Y: 175,
            line3X: 80, line3Y: 250
        })}, 150);
    },
    growVertical = function() {

        if (height < 100 || width < 200) {
            if (height < 100) {
                context.beginPath();
                context.moveTo(pos.up.x, pos.up.y);
                context.lineTo(pos.up.x, pos.up.y - 2);
                context.moveTo(pos.down.x, pos.down.y);
                context.lineTo(pos.down.x, pos.down.y + 2);
                context.stroke();
                context.closePath();

                height = height + 2;
                pos.up.y = pos.up.y - 2;
                pos.down.y = pos.down.y + 2;
            }
            if (width < 200) {
                context.beginPath();
                context.moveTo(pos.left.x, pos.left.y);
                context.lineTo(pos.left.x - 2, pos.left.y);
                context.moveTo(pos.right.x, pos.right.y);
                context.lineTo(pos.right.x + 2, pos.right.y);
                context.stroke();
                context.closePath();

                width = width + 2
                pos.left.x = pos.left.x - 2;
                pos.right.x = pos.right.x + 2;
            }
        } else {
            clearInterval(crossInt);
            addStripes();
        }

    },
    crossInt = setInterval( function() { growVertical() }, 1);
},
```

What just happened?

Again, we have an outer inline function (called `redCross()`) containing some properties that set the color and line styles, and some nested functions that will be used to draw the red cross and the four custom shapes. As with the previous function, we declare the `width` and `height` control variables, and an object called `pos` containing the starting positions for the lines that make up the cross. The cross is drawn first with the `growVertical()` function.

This function is very similar to the function in the last section of code. We draw four lines starting in the middle of the rectangle which radiate to the top and bottom-center, and the right and left-center.

The four custom shapes are drawn using a single master function that accepts a configuration object specifying the start point (passed to the `moveTo()` method), and the points that make up each subpath (passed to the `lineTo()` methods). We then use the `setTimeout` JavaScript function to create each shape one after the other, using the object passed to the master function to specify the relevant points on the canvas to draw each shape.

This is all the code we need; so now when we run the page, we should see the animation of the flag being drawn. The code works in all browsers, with varying levels of performance for each browser. Animating the `<canvas>` element is all about conditional `if` statements, intervals, and timeouts. As we saw, the code itself is quite straightforward. We just need rather a lot of it in order to produce even simple animations.

Pop quiz – animating the canvas

Q1. Why did we store each call to `setInterval()` in a variable?

1. For performance reasons
2. In order to clear the interval when appropriate
3. Because of the closure created with the anonymous function as the first argument to the function
4. So that we can pass arguments to the function called by the interval

Q2. In the first function, where we drew the blue rectangle, we set the width of the `<canvas>` element each time the `rectMotion()` function is called by the interval. Why?

1. To make sure the `<canvas>` element was big enough to contain the rectangle as it grew
2. To correct a bug in Internet Explorer
3. To reset the state of the `<canvas>` element, ensuring there was only one rectangle at each point in the animation
4. As a requirement for setting the `fillStyle` property

Have a go hero – creating canvas animations

Go back to the static version of the flag you drew of your home country (or the logo or image of your choice), and convert it so that the different parts of the flag are animated and brought into existence.

Creating a canvas game

The best animations are those that are interactive and engage the user, and this is exactly how a game can be seen, as one continuous, user-driven animation. The power of the `<canvas>` element is best demonstrated when it is used to create games, as we'll see over the course of this section.

We'll create a very basic clone of the arcade classic *Space Invaders* with a series of alien ships that slowly advance down the screen, and a user-controlled space ship at the bottom that can shoot the incoming aliens:

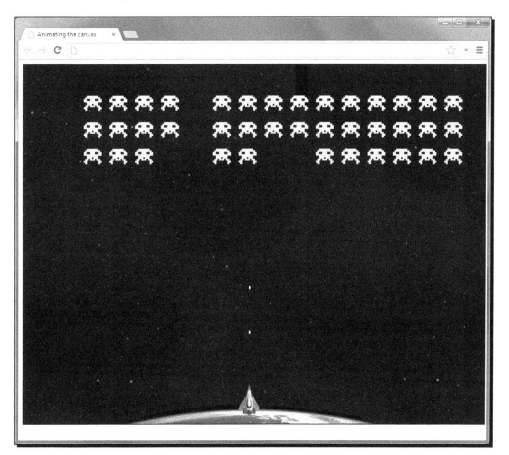

Time for action – creating the initial page

The initial page that we'll use for this example is similar to that used in the previous example:

1. Create a new page in your text editor that contains the following markup:

```
<!DOCTYPE html>
<html lang="en">
  <head>
    <meta charset="utf-8">
    <title>A canvas and jQuery Game</title>
    <link rel="stylesheet" href="css/canvas-game.css">
  </head>
  <body>
    <canvas tabindex="1" id="c" width="900" height="675">
      <p>Your browser doesn't support the canvas element!</p>
    </canvas>
    <script src="js/jquery.js"></script>
    <script>
      $(function() {

      });
    </script>
  </body>
</html>
```

2. Save the file as `canvas-game.html`. We also require a very basic stylesheet for our game. All we're styling is the `<canvas>` element itself. Create a new stylesheet containing the following style rules:

```
canvas {
  border:1px solid #000;
  margin:auto;
  display:block;
  outline:none;
  background:url(../img/bg.gif) no-repeat;
}
```

3. Save this file in the `css` directory as `canvas-game.css`.

What just happened?

The main element on the page is of course the `<canvas>` element. The only difference between this and the element used in previous examples is that we have set the `tabindex` attribute on it so that it can receive keyboard events, which is necessary for detecting and reacting to the input from the user. We're also using jQuery in this example and using the standard anonymous function and the `$` aliasing construct we've used throughout the book.

The styles we've used simply position the `<canvas>` element in the center of the page, give it a border, and remove the dotted outline that appears around focused elements in some browsers. We also set a background image on the element.

The background image applied to the `<canvas>` element helps to set a scene for our game, and using CSS to set a background image on the `<canvas>` element is much easier than drawing the image within it.

Time for action – creating the initial script

The script for the game is quite long, so we'll look at it in different sections, starting with the initial structure of the script. The following code should go into the anonymous function at the bottom of the page:

```
var canvas = document.getElementById("c"),
  context = canvas.getContext("2d"),
  motionInt = null,
  dirCounter = 0,
  alienSpeed = 1000,
  aliens = [],
  alienMotion = function(dir) {

  },

  addAliens = function() {

  },

  ship = new Image(),
  shipPos = [430, 600];

  ship.src = "img/ship.png";
  ship.onload = function() {

  context.drawImage(ship, shipPos[0], shipPos[1]);

  addAliens();

  };
```

What just happened?

Essentially, all we've done here is define a series of variables and an onload event handler. The canvas and context variables are defined first, as in previous examples, in order to access and manipulate the canvas.

We also set a variable called motionInt, which will be used to hold the ID of a setInterval() function later on, a variable called dirCounter which will be used to determine which direction the aliens move in, an alienSpeed variable to set the speed that the aliens move at, and an empty aliens array which we'll use to keep track of each alien on the page.

Following this we define two inline functions, one to move the aliens and one to add the aliens to the page. These are empty at the moment but we'll populate each of them next. We also create a new image, which will be the user-controlled space ship, and a shipPosition array which will be used to keep track of the ship's location on the page.

Once we've defined all our variables, we set the src of the new image object we created to represent the space ship. We then attach an onload event handler to the ship object, which will be executed once the image has finished loading. Within this function, we draw the ship on the canvas using the values stored in the imagePosition array. We then call the addAliens() function, which will add the aliens to the canvas. We can add the code to the addAliens() function next.

Time for action – adding the aliens to the page

Replace the addAliens() inline function in the previous code block with the following code:

```
addAliens = function() {

  var alienPos = [13, 0],
  alien = new Image();

  alien.src = "img/alien.gif";
  alien.onload = function () {
    for (var x = 0; x < 15; x++) {
      for (var y = 0; y < 3; y++) {


        context.drawImage(alien, alienPos[0], alienPos[1]);

        var data = {
          img: alien, posX: alienPos[0], posY: alienPos[1]
        };
```

```
         aliens.push(data);
         if (alienPos[1] < 100) {
           alienPos[1] = alienPos[1] + 50;
         } else {
           alienPos[0] = alienPos[0] + 50;
           alienPos[1] = 0;
         }
       };
     }
   };

   motionInt = setInterval(function () {
     alienMotion("right"); }, alienSpeed);
  },
```

What just happened?

We first define a new array that we'll use to incrementally set the position of each alien ship while the aliens are initially being drawn to the canvas. We define a new Image object for the image that will be used by all of the alien ships and set its src attribute. We then set an onload handler for the new alien image so that we can manipulate the image once it has finished loading.

We want to create three rows of 15 aliens, so within the onload handler, we start with two nested for loops where the outer loop runs 15 times and on each loop, the inner for loop executes three times. Within the nested loops, we first draw the new alien to the canvas using the values stored in the alienPos array. We then create a new data object which stores a reference to the image object, and the x and y position of the image on the canvas. The new data object is then pushed into the aliens array which we defined earlier at the start of the script.

We then update the values in the alienPos array. If the second item in the array (the item with an index of 1) is less than 100, we add 50 to the value of the array item. The second item in the array corresponds to the position on the y axis of the canvas. This will give us a single column of three aliens. Note that we start the x position of the first three aliens at 13 instead of 0 so that there is a gutter between the edge of the canvas and the first column of aliens.

If the second array item is more than 100, we add 50 to the first item in the array instead, which corresponds to the x axis on the canvas, and reset the second array item to zero. This will give us 15 columns of three aliens.

Once all of the aliens have been drawn on the canvas, we set an interval that will repeatedly execute the next function, `alienMotion()`, according to the number of milliseconds contained in the `alienSpeed` variable, which is initially set to `1000` at the start of the script. The interval ID is stored in the `motionInt` variable we also created at the start of the script. We can add the code to our `alienMotion()` function next.

Time for action – moving the aliens

Our next block of code will give the aliens their motion, causing them to advance to the right along the canvas first, then down a line, then to the left, and so on and so forth. Replace the `alienMotion()` function we previously defined with the following code:

```
alienMotion = function (dir) {

  var alienLength = aliens.length;

  if (dirCounter < 4) {

    for (var x = 0; x < alienLength; x++) {
      context.clearRect(aliens[x].posX, aliens[x].posY,
        aliens[x].img.width, aliens[x].img.height);
    }

    for (var y = 0; y < alienLength; y++) {
      aliens[y].posX = (dir === "right") ?  aliens[y].posX + 35 :
        aliens[y].posX - 35;

    context.drawImage(aliens[y].img, aliens[y].posX,
      aliens[y].posY);
    }

    dirCounter++;
  } else {
    clearInterval(motionInt);
    dirCounter = 0;

    for (var z = 0; z < alienLength; z++) {
      context.clearRect(aliens[z].posX, aliens[z].posY,
        aliens[z].img.width, aliens[z].img.height);
    }

    if (aliens[alienLength - 1].posY > 530) {
      canvas.width = 900;
```

```
      context.fillStyle = "#fff";
      context.textAlign = "center";
      context.font = "bold 36px Tahoma";
      context.fillText("GAME OVER!", 450, 350);
      $(canvas).blur().unbind("keydown");
    } else {

      for (var a = 0; a < alienLength; a++) {
        aliens[a].posY = aliens[a].posY + 29;

        context.drawImage(aliens[a].img, aliens[a].posX,
          aliens[a].posY);
      }

      motionInt = (dir === "right") ? setInterval(
        function () { alienMotion("left"); }, alienSpeed) :
        setInterval(function () { alienMotion("right"); },
        alienSpeed);
    }
  }
},
```

What just happened?

The first thing we do is store the length of the aliens array in a local variable. We'll use several `for` loops in this function, so it makes sense to retrieve this value only once and compare the counter variables of the `for` loops to the variable instead of checking the length on each iteration of the various loops.

We then use an `if` statement to check whether the `dirCounter` variable is less than 4. Remember, this was one of the variables we set at the start of the script. If the variable is less than 4, we first use a `for` loop to cycle through each item in the `aliens` array and use the `clearRect()` function to remove the alien from the canvas.

We then use a second `for` loop that cycles through the `aliens` array once more, this time updating the x position of each alien by either adding or removing 35 from the current x position stored in the current item in the array.

Whether 35 is added or removed is determined by the parameter passed into the function. The first time the `alienMotion()` function is called, it will receive the parameter `right`, so the aliens will initially move across to the canvas to the right. We then draw each alien in its new position. Once the `for` loop has finished and all of the aliens have been drawn in their new positions, we update the `dirCounter` variable.

If the `dirCounter` variable is equal to 4, the aliens have moved horizontally across the canvas as far as they should, so this time we need to move the aliens down the canvas line instead of across it. In this branch of the condition, we clear the interval that controls the horizontal movement, then reset the `dirCounter` variable back to 0. We then remove the aliens from the canvas by clearing the rectangle that each alien covers.

Before moving the aliens down a line, we first check whether the y position of the last alien in the array is greater than 530, as this is the maximum distance from the top of the canvas that an alien should get. If it is greater than this figure, at least one alien has reached the bottom of the canvas and it's game over for the player.

In this case, we clear the whole canvas, removing the space ship and any surviving aliens, and print the text **GAME OVER!** on the center of the canvas. We also use jQuery to unbind the keyboard events that control the space ship (we'll add these bindings shortly).

If the aliens have not reached the bottom of the canvas, we instead use another `for` loop to iterate over each alien in the array and move each of their y positions down by one line, and then draw each alien in its new location.

We then set a new interval, passing the string in the opposite direction to the `alienMotion()` function that was used previously. These loops of four steps, to the right, one step down, four steps to the left, and so on, will continue until the aliens reach the bottom of the canvas and the game is over. Next, we need to add the handlers that enable the player to control the space ship.

Time for action – adding handlers to control the ship

The following block of code should replace the `onload` event handler for the ship image object:

```
ship.onload = function () {

  context.drawImage(ship, shipPos[0], shipPos[1]);

  addAliens();
  $(canvas).focus().bind("keydown", function (e) {

    if (e.which === 37 || e.which === 39) {

      context.clearRect(shipPos[0], shipPos[1], ship.width,
        ship.height);

      if (e.which === 37 && shipPos[0] > 4) {
        shipPos[0] = shipPos[0] - 4;
      } else if (e.which === 39 && shipPos[0] < 896 - ship.width) {
```

```
            shipPos[0] = shipPos[0] + 4;
        }

        context.drawImage(ship, shipPos[0], shipPos[1]);
    } else if (e.which === 32) {
        context.fillStyle = "#fff";
        var bulletPos = shipPos[0] + 20,
            newBulletPos = [bulletPos, 596],
            alienLength = aliens.length,
            fire = function () {
                if (newBulletPos[1] > 0) {
                    context.clearRect(newBulletPos[0],
                        newBulletPos[1], 3, 6);
                    newBulletPos[1] = newBulletPos[1] - 2;
                    context.fillRect(newBulletPos[0], newBulletPos[1], 3, 6);

                    for (var x = 0; x < alienLength; x++) {
                        if (newBulletPos[1] === aliens[x].posY ||
                            newBulletPos[1] === aliens[x].posY +
                            aliens[x].img.height) {
                        if (newBulletPos[0] > aliens[x].posX &&
                            newBulletPos[0] - aliens[x].posX <
                            aliens[x].img.width + 13) {
                            context.clearRect(aliens[x].posX, aliens[x].posY,
                                aliens[x].img.width, aliens[x].img.height);
                            aliens.splice(x, 1);
                            clearInterval(bulletInt);
                            context.clearRect(newBulletPos[0],
                                newBulletPos[1], 3, 6);
                            if (!aliens.length) {
                                clearInterval(motionInt);
                                dirCounter = 0;
                                alienSpeed = alienSpeed - 100;
                                addAliens();
                            }
                        }
                    }
                }
            } else {
                context.clearRect(newBulletPos[0], newBulletPos[1], 3, 6);
                clearInterval(bulletInt);
            }
        },
        bulletInt = setInterval(function () { fire(); }, 1);
    }
});
};
```

What just happened?

We use jQuery to attach an event handler to the `<canvas>` element that listens for the `keydown` events. Although we're not providing support for IE and so don't need jQuery for its cross-browser normalization when attaching events, it still makes the event handling process much easier.

Within the function that is executed whenever a `keydown` event is detected, we check for the presence of either the left or right arrow keys, which have a `which` property in the event object of `37` and `39`, or the spacebar, which has the code `32`.

If the code `37` or `39` is detected, we then use a nested `if` statement to determine between the two keys. We also check that the ship hasn't reached either the left edge, or the right edge of the canvas.

We then use the `clearRect()` function to remove the ship and draw a new one either 4 pixels to the left, or 4 pixels to the right depending on which key was pressed. This gives the ship left and right motion along the bottom of the canvas.

The second branch of the outer conditional deals with the spacebar being pressed, which causes a bullet to leave the ship and travel in a straight line to the top of the canvas. The bullets will be white, so we set the `fillStyle` property of the canvas to `#fff`.

We also declare some more local variables here including `bulletPos`, which is the current position of the bullet plus half of the width of the ship, and an array to hold the x and y coordinates of the bullet. The values for this array are set to the `bulletPos` variable for the x position, and directly above the nose of the ship for the y position. We also store the length of the aliens array as a local variable for use in a `for` loop once again.

We define an inline function along with our variables called `fire()`. This function is used in conjunction with an interval to create the motion of the bullet. Within this function, we check that the bullet hasn't reached the top of the canvas, and provided it hasn't, that is, if its y position is greater than 0, we remove the bullet with the `clearRect()` function, then update the values in the `bulletPos` array and draw the bullet in its new location using the updated values from the array.

Once the position of the bullet has been updated, we then need to check whether the bullet, in its new position, has collided with an alien or not, so we use a `for` loop to iterate over each alien in the aliens array.

On each iteration, we first check whether the bullet falls within the y axis of an alien, that is, whether its position is less than the bottom edge of an alien, but more than its top edge. The aliens are positioned according to their top-left corner, so to work out whether the bullet has passed its bottom edge we just add the height of an alien to its y position.

If the bullet does fall within the alien on the y axis, we then check whether it falls within the space an alien is taking up along the x axis. If it does, we remove the alien from the canvas with the `clearRect()` function and splice the alien out of the array so that it stays removed.

We then remove the bullet from the canvas using the `clearRect()` function again, and clear the `bulletInt` interval. If there are no more aliens left, we clear the interval producing the motion of the aliens, reset the `dirCounter` variable, reduce the `alienSpeed` variable by `100`, and then call the `addAliens()` function to redraw the aliens at the top of the canvas.

This is effectively how the player moves up to the next level, and each time the aliens are redrawn they move faster, creating basic progression of the game. This now brings us to the end of the code. If we run the game now in a standard-compliant browser, such as Firefox or Chrome, we should find that we have a perfectly playable game, implemented entirely using JavaScript and the `<canvas>` element.

Pop quiz – creating canvas-based games

Q1. In this example, a lot of features related to the player's space ship was put into an `onload` event handler. Why?

1. Because we cannot interact with an image until it has loaded completely
2. To make the code work correctly in Internet Explorer
3. Because the code runs faster once the image has finished loading
4. To help make our code more modular

Q2. Why did we set the `textAlign` property of the canvas to center when writing the **GAME OVER!** message?

1. Setting the alignment is a prerequisite for writing text to the canvas
2. Because it is easier than working out the width of the text and then setting its position on the x axis in order to position the text in the center of the canvas
3. To anti-alias the text
4. Because it is more efficient than using padding

Have a go hero – extending the space invaders clone

Our game is a much simpler version of the original space invaders. The original arcade game had many other features including aliens that fired back at the player's ship, bases to hide behind, and one-off special aliens that appeared randomly throughout the game and dropped bonuses when hit.

Certainly, one thing that the game needs is a scoring mechanism; otherwise there is simply no incentive to play. Implement a scoring system that tracks a player's score throughout the game and saves the highest score to the player's machine. This could be done easily with jQuery and the cookie plugin, or using LocalStorage.

I'd also urge you, as this is the last example of the book, to implement some of the other missing features, such as giving the aliens the ability to fire back and adding bases or shields that the player can hide beneath when the going gets tough.

Summary

In this chapter, we looked at the HTML5 `<canvas>` element and saw how it can be used to create simple and static images, basic animations, and even complex interactive games. It provides a rich API that allows us to interact with it programmatically and gives us complete pixel-level control over an area of the page.

In this chapter, we covered the `HTMLCanvasElement` interface, drawing to the `<canvas>` element, creating animations on the `<canvas>` element, and we also created an interactive game with the `<canvas>` element. Like with the CSS3 examples from the last chapter, there are no methods or properties in jQuery specifically for use with `<canvas>`, although there has been a number of plugins that combine the power of `<canvas>` with the ease of jQuery, and several projects that extend the jQuery's `animate()` method to allow it work on objects drawn to the canvas. For more information on this, a good starting point is Steven Wittens' blog at `http://acko.net/blog/abusing-jquery-animate-for-fun-and-profit-and-bacon`.

We've now reached the end of the book. I hope that over these 10 chapters, I've given you a solid foundation for producing animations using jQuery that acts as a solid starting point for you to bring your web-based UIs to life.

Pop Quiz Answers

Chapter 1, Getting Started

Pop quiz – basic animation with jQuery

Q1	2
Q2	3

Chapter 2, Image Animation

Pop quiz – using fadeIn()

Q1	3
Q2	1

Pop quiz – length() and milliseconds

Q1	2
Q2	3

Pop quiz – preventDefault() and setInterval()

Q1	2
Q2	2

Pop quiz – altering variables and zero index

Q1	4
Q2	1

Chapter 3, Background Animation

Pop quiz – chaining with the animate() method

Q1	3

Pop quiz – the scroll() and scrollTop() methods

Q1	2
Q2	2

Chapter 4, Navigation Animation

Pop quiz – the ^ symbol and the stop() method

Q1	3
Q2	1

Chapter 5, Form and Input Animation

Pop quiz – form animation and jQuery UI

Q1	4
Q2	2

Chapter 6, Extended Animations with jQuery UI

Pop quiz – using the effect of API

Q1	4
Q2	2

Pop quiz – using show/hide logic

Q1	3
Q2	1

Pop quiz – using easing

Q1	2
Q2	1

Pop quiz – easing, color, and class animation

Q1	4
Q2	3

Chapter 7, Custom Animations

Pop quiz – creating an animated content-viewer

Q1	2
Q2	3

Pop quiz – creating expanding images

Q1	4
Q2	1

Pop quiz – creating a plugin

Q1	4
Q2	3

Chapter 8, Other Popular Animations

Pop quiz – implementing proximity animations

Q1	3
Q2	2

Pop quiz – creating a marquee scroller

Q1	4

Chapter 9, CSS3 Animations

Pop quiz – implementing CSS3 rotation

Q1	3
Q2	1

Pop quiz – using the matrix

Q1	3
Q2	4

Chapter 10, Canvas Animations

Pop quiz – drawing to the canvas

Q1	4
Q2	3

Pop quiz – animating the canvas

Q1	2
Q2	3

Pop quiz – creating canvas-based games

Q1	1
Q2	2

Index

G

getContext(a) method
  using 228
getContext() method 237
getElementById() method 237
getImageData(a, b, c, d) method 233
getJSON() method 187-189
get() method 207, 216
getVendor() function 208, 215
globalAlpha property 229
globalCompositeOperation property 229
goAnim() function 174, 176
growDiagonal() function 243
growVertical() function 243-246

H

header element 179
height parameter 128, 147
height property 234
hidden class 134
hide() method 11
highlight effect
  about 84
  applying 84-86
  configuration options 84
Hoisting 214
hover class 58
hover() function 32
hover() method 57, 94, 115
hover style
  extending 58
href attribute 60, 117
HTMLCanvasElement interface
  <canvas> element, using 228
  context methods 228, 229
  images, drawing 231, 232
  learning 228
  native shapes 229, 230
  patterns, drawing 231, 232
  pixels, manipulating 233, 234
  shape, drawing with path 230, 231
  text strings, writing 232
  transformation methods, applying 232, 233
html() method 36, 146

I

id attribute 133, 144, 172, 228
illusion of depth
  creating, parallax effect used 42
image animation 21
imageData object 233, 234
Image object 251
image rotator
  scripting 26-28
images
  drawing, to canvas 231
  full size, defining 143, 144
  small size, defining 143, 144
img element 207
index() method 63
init() function 240
Initiate the action button 15
innerText element 172
Internet Explorer 9 (IE9) 13
is() method 177

J

join() method 208
jQuery
  animating with 11, 12
  URL 11
jQuery animation plugin
  creating 150
  jQuery animation pluginUI, creating 157
  style, adding 150-152
  test page, creating 150-152
jQuery() function 155
jQuery.fx.interval property 12
jQuery.fx.off property 12
jQuery methods
  chaining together 41, 42
jQuery namespace
  plugin method, adding to 154, 155
jQuery object 150
jQuery UI
  about 77
  animations, adding 80-98
  class transitions 122, 123
  color animations 121, 122
  new template file, creating 79

Thank you for buying
jQuery 2.0 Animation Techniques Beginner's Guide

About Packt Publishing

Packt, pronounced 'packed', published its first book "*Mastering phpMyAdmin for Effective MySQL Management*" in April 2004 and subsequently continued to specialize in publishing highly focused books on specific technologies and solutions.

Our books and publications share the experiences of your fellow IT professionals in adapting and customizing today's systems, applications, and frameworks. Our solution based books give you the knowledge and power to customize the software and technologies you're using to get the job done. Packt books are more specific and less general than the IT books you have seen in the past. Our unique business model allows us to bring you more focused information, giving you more of what you need to know, and less of what you don't.

Packt is a modern, yet unique publishing company, which focuses on producing quality, cutting-edge books for communities of developers, administrators, and newbies alike. For more information, please visit our website: www.packtpub.com.

About Packt Open Source

In 2010, Packt launched two new brands, Packt Open Source and Packt Enterprise, in order to continue its focus on specialization. This book is part of the Packt Open Source brand, home to books published on software built around Open Source licences, and offering information to anybody from advanced developers to budding web designers. The Open Source brand also runs Packt's Open Source Royalty Scheme, by which Packt gives a royalty to each Open Source project about whose software a book is sold.

Writing for Packt

We welcome all inquiries from people who are interested in authoring. Book proposals should be sent to author@packtpub.com. If your book idea is still at an early stage and you would like to discuss it first before writing a formal book proposal, contact us; one of our commissioning editors will get in touch with you.

We're not just looking for published authors; if you have strong technical skills but no writing experience, our experienced editors can help you develop a writing career, or simply get some additional reward for your expertise.

jQuery Game Development Essentials

ISBN: 978-1-84969-506-0   Paperback: 244 pages

Learn how to make fun and addictive multi-platform games using jQuery

1. Discover how you can create a fantastic RPG, arcade game, or platformer using jQuery!

2. Learn how you can integrate your game with various social networks, creating multiplayer experiences and also ensuring compatibility with mobile devices

3. Create your very own framework, harnessing the very best design patterns and proven techniques along the way

Instant jQuery Boilerplate for Plugins

ISBN: 978-1-84951-970-0   Paperback: 82 pages

Get started with jQuery plugin development with this rapid-paced guide

1. Learn something new in an Instant! A short, fast, focused guide delivering immediate results

2. Build your first basic jQuery Plugin

3. Learn how to make your plugin configurable

4. Get to grips with the structure of jQuery Boilerplate

Please check **www.PacktPub.com** for information on our titles